S0-BDO-303

Year-Round House Care

OTHER BOOKS IN THE HOMEOWNER'S LIBRARY SERIES

Home Security

Floors, Walls & Ceilings

Preventive Home Maintenance

Creative Ideas for Household Storage

THE HOMEOWNER'S LIBRARY

Year-Round House Care

A Seasonal Checklist for Basic Home Maintenance

Graham Blackburn and the Editors of Consumer Reports Books

CONSUMER REPORTS BOOKS
A DIVISION OF CONSUMERS UNION
MOUNT VERNON, NEW YORK

Copyright © 1991 by Graham Blackburn and Consumers Union
of the United States, Inc., Mount Vernon, New York 10553.
All rights reserved, including the right of reproduction in whole
or in part in any form.

Library of Congress Cataloging-in-Publication Data
Blackburn, Graham, 1940–
Year-round house care: a seasonal checklist for basic home
maintenance/Graham Blackburn and the editors of Consumer Reports
Books.
p. cm.—(The Homeowner's library)
Includes index.
ISBN 0-89043-352-6
1. Dwellings—Maintenance and repair—Amateurs' manuals.
I. Consumer Reports Books. II. Title. III. Series.
TH4817.B554 1991
643'.7—dc20 90-47255
CIP
Rev.

Design by The Sarabande Press
Illustrations by Graham Blackburn
First Printing, March 1991
Manufactured in the United States of America

Originally published in 1981 by Richard Marek Publishers under the title *An Illustrated Calendar of Home Repair.* This edition has been revised and updated.

Year-Round House Care is a Consumer Reports Book published by Consumers Union, the nonprofit organization that publishes *Consumer Reports,* the monthly magazine of test reports, product Ratings, and buying guidance. Established in 1936, Consumers Union is chartered under the Not-for-Profit Corporation Law of the State of New York.

The purposes of Consumers Union, as stated in its charter, are to provide consumers with information and counsel on consumer goods and services, to give information on all matters relating to the expenditure of the family income, and to initiate and to cooperate with individual and group efforts seeking to create and maintain decent living standards.

Consumers Union derives its income solely from the sale of *Consumer Reports* and other publications. In addition, expenses of occasional public service efforts may be met, in part, by nonrestrictive, noncommercial contributions, grants, and fees. Consumers Union accepts no advertising or product samples and is not beholden in any way to any commercial interest. Its Ratings and reports are solely for the use of the readers of its publications. Neither the Ratings, nor the reports, nor any Consumers Union publications, including this book, may be used in advertising or for any commercial purpose. Consumers Union will take all steps open to it to prevent such uses of its materials, its name, or the name of *Consumer Reports.*

Contents

Introduction

> Now, if your buildings have been neglected, and are all dilapidated, if you have chosen rather to sit by the fire and count your fingers than to take the hammer and drive a few nails; or if you have been in the habit of hanging round Peter Fogo's grog-shop, to the disregard of your home affairs, then you are indeed a sufferer.
>
> Whew! how the wind blows! Crack, slap, rip up and tear all! Your old hovel is about taking its departure amidst the posting winds.
>
> From *The Old Farmer's Almanac*
> published in New England, 1835

Some homeowners delight in puttering around the house and tinkering with things. A few might even enjoy coping with the occasional household emergency. But most of us hope that we won't have to deal with many crises in a house, and subscribe happily to the maxim "if it ain't broke, don't fix it!" Our lives are much too busy as it is without looking for extra work, especially in areas that may be largely a mystery to us. Unfortunately, however, the inner workings of a house are composed of vital systems which, if ignored, can break down and present us with precisely those emergencies we hope to avoid.

The secret of a secure, comfortable house lies in regular maintenance. This does not mean you must spend hours every week with tools in hand. For the most part, all that is required is a fairly knowledgeable inspection of house and premises conducted at the right time. Knowing what to look for and when, together with doing the few small maintenance chores that are unavoidable, can keep your house snug and weatherproof, and help you spot those troubled areas that may need professional attention.

To the new homeowner, maintaining even a small house may seem a daunting prospect. Facing him or her are an overwhelming number of complicated parts: the basic structure, which includes deep mysteries like the foundation and bearing walls; the plumbing, with its maze of largely hidden pipes; the electrical system, certainly unknown territory for the newcomer; and the heating and cooling systems, which remain largely forgotten until they break down on a cold winter's night or on a sweltering summer day. A larger house presents even more complex features to the apprehensive owner. But even the most unwilling do-it-yourselfer can manage to keep things under control by reducing the systems to simple, easily inspected units that can be addressed in an orderly fashion twice a year or so.

Year-Round House Care does exactly that. A basic guide to regular house checkups, it leads you step-by-step through many of the structures that compose your home, showing you what to look for and when. It will help you organize what has to be done on a seasonal basis throughout the year and will serve as a reminder for those routine chores that accompany the change of seasons.

Each chapter deals with a specific area of the house, one best attended to at a particular time. The most important aspects of each area are pinpointed and discussed, making it easy for you to follow the instructions for any requisite light maintenance. If you encounter anything more serious, you should be able to deal with the problem or realize, before it becomes an emergency, that professional help is necessary.

Not every detail covered in this book is relevant to every dwelling, but the information found here is important to the continued structural health and good appearance of almost every type of house, whether traditional or contemporary, in every section of the country.

A NOTE ABOUT THE PRODUCT RATINGS

Ratings from *Consumer Reports* on a number of home maintenance products are an added feature of this book and can be found in the appendix. The Ratings offer comparative buying information that greatly increases the likelihood you will receive value for your money.

In the Ratings charts, products are usually listed in order of estimated quality, which means Consumers Union's technical staff judged the brand listed first to be the best, the one listed next to be second best, and so on. Whenever rated products are considered to be about equal to one another, they are listed in a special fashion, for example, alphabetically and within brackets.

Each Ratings chart has a notation of the month and year in which the Ratings appeared in *Consumer Reports*. Usually the prices are listed as published at the time of the original report. When you shop for one of these products, consider the list price only as a guide, since discounts are widely available and prices may have gone up since the report was published.

Keep in mind, too, that manufacturers commonly change products every year or so in order to keep up with the competition, to stimulate sales, or to incorporate technological improvements. Unfortunately, dealer inventories don't always keep pace with such rapid changes, and older models are carried over long after newer ones have been introduced. As a result, older models may remain available for months or even years after they have been discontinued.

Even though the particular brand and model of maintenance equipment you select from the Ratings may be out of stock or superseded by a later version, the information given can be of great help in sorting out products and their characteristics.

PART I

Spring and Summer

ONE

Postwinter Cleanup

Even in the warmer sections of the country, the arrival of spring is a noticeable event. There may be no snow to melt and no ice to thaw, but the natives can tell by signs often invisible to people from colder areas. The rains stop; the temperature begins to rise; and plants begin to grow again. All at once the out-of-doors looks different; even the air has a different quality.

For the rest of the country, the arrival of spring is a more dramatic event. The snow, if any, disappears; the gray hue of soil and sky fade; and suddenly there are colors—yellow forsythia, red quince in bloom, and green grass once more.

For the homeowner though, whether in the North or South, this is not the time to sit back comfortably and watch the transition. There are important cleaning-up chores to be done.

WHERE TO START

As the snow disappears and the winds of March begin to die, the homeowner begins to pay more attention to the condition of the grounds. Although the lawn may still be too soggy to deal with, gardeners can remove the mulch from spring bulbs and prune their fruit trees. Trellises should be repaired and painted, if necessary, before they begin to be covered by vines and climbing plants; dead limbs of bushes and small trees should be removed as well. Once the ground hardens, it's time to clear up in general—pick up broken branches, clear walks, and so forth. (Those broken branches, snapped in two and placed neatly to dry in a decorative basket by the fireplace, make good kindling for next winter's fires.)

This period of rapid climatic change can also uncover some potentially serious exterior problems, such as an inadequate or malfunctioning drainage system.

DRAINAGE SYSTEMS

Ideally, at the time of its original construction, your house should have had an underground system of drainage installed around the foundation to lead water away from the building. If it did not, or if the effectiveness of such a system has become impaired, a number of unpleasant things can happen. Most likely, you will find water seeping into the basement after heavy spring rains or a thaw; you may even find that the house gradually is surrounded by a moat or a marsh. In freezing weather, this collected water can expand and cause the ground to heave, possibly damaging underground pipes and wires, destroying paths and steps, pushing plants out of the ground, and even, in the worst-case scenario, causing foundations to collapse.

The well-sited house is positioned atop a dry, well-drained rise of ground. But not all houses are so well situated; many are built on some kind of slope. This type of situation can provide a built-in drainage problem, at least on one side of the house. Even more

FIGURE 1.1 *Drainage problems*

FIGURE 1.2 *Good and bad sites*

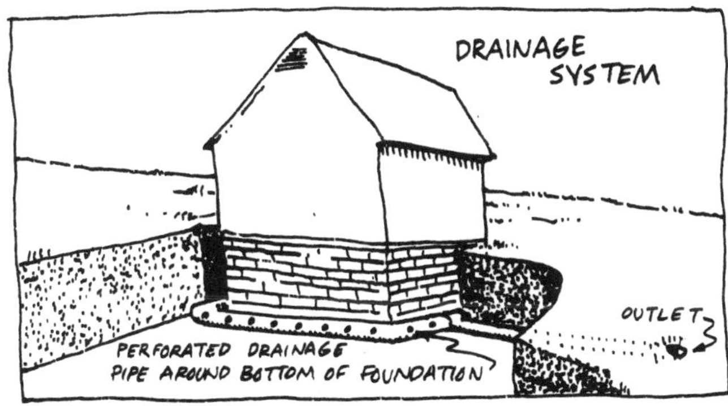

FIGURE 1.3 *Drainage system*

problematic is a house built in a depression or adjoining a marsh or in an area with a high water table.

Nevertheless, wherever the house may be, it should have been the builder's duty to provide an adequate drainage system. Because the drainage system is buried next to the foundation, it is difficult to service. Indeed, if it fails, the only cure may involve excavation and replacement. It is important, therefore, to know how to recognize the symptoms of an incipient breakdown in this vital area.

One good indication, of course, is standing or seeping water in the basement after heavy rains. Another is pools of standing water next to the house after a downpour. The exact causes of this condition may not be readily apparent, so you may have to call in professional help to find the problem and rectify the situation.

One of the first things to check for is whether the gutters and downspouts are doing their job properly—carrying water off the roof and away from the house, perhaps to a dry well in the ground. A dry well is often a necessary part of the drainage system if your land is sloping or if there are other potential water problems. If the gutter-downspout system is not working properly, it can overload the ground next to the house with so much water that even a good foundation drainage system cannot drain it away (see page 29).

Perhaps the most common problem with the foundation drainage system itself is the infiltration and blocking of the drainage pipes or tiles by the roots of neighboring trees and shrubs. Some species, allowed to grow too close to the house, are worse than others. Maples, for example, are infamous in this regard, and their roots seem to seek out drainage pipes as a perfect water supply for their thirst. (When planting a tree, it pays to remember that the root system of a mature tree can be as extensive as its crown.)

The lay of the land can cause problems, too. If the ground is not sufficiently sloped away from the house, a catchment basin is gradually formed by the water running down the slope, where it collects. To compound the problem, waterlogged ground freezes faster than well-

FIGURE 1.4 *Section of drainage pipe and connector*

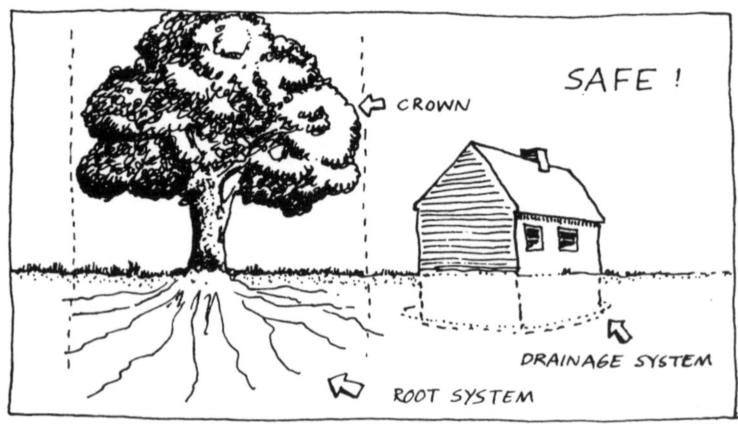

FIGURE 1.5 *Root system of large tree*

drained ground, and once it is frozen traps more water (which cannot seep down to the drainage tiles below). The cure for this situation is to grade the earth away from the house, provide a secondary drainage tile near the surface, and even dig a small ditch to carry away surface water.

Another solution for an area that doesn't drain properly and is too wet or heaves badly in cold weather (because of the excessive moisture in the ground turning to frost) is to add a porch to that side of the house so that the problem area simply doesn't get as wet. This stratagem may sound extreme, but the combination of solving a

FIGURE 1.6 *Catchment basin*

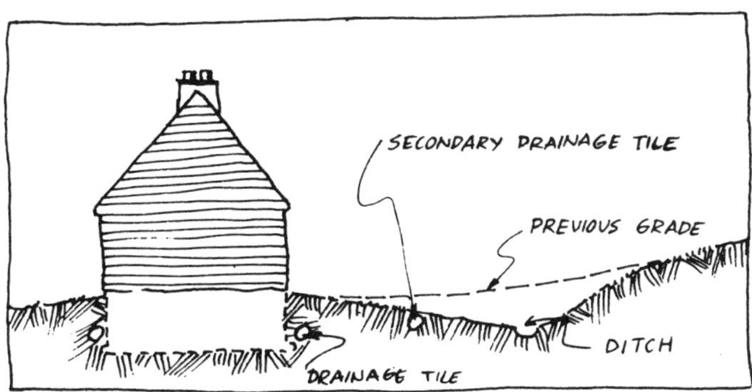

FIGURE 1.7 *Regrading*

FIGURE 1.8 *Added porch*

vexing problem and acquiring an extension of your living space may be irresistible. If your space and finances permit, it's worth considering.

If, after a professional appraisal, it turns out that the problem requires major excavation or moving earth, it might be best to do the work in the drier months of summer. (Remember, though, it is sometimes difficult to recall how serious a problem was after time has passed and the symptoms have temporarily disappeared.)

Culverts and Ditches

After the snows have gone and before the rainy season begins is the time to take care of another job related to site drainage: checking that any ditch or culvert running around the house—or along or under the driveway—is still intact and clear. These culverts are designed to carry off major runoffs during heavy rains.

In areas of measurable snowfall, where snowplowing is necessary, culverts and ditches can suffer many mishaps. These often pass unnoticed until, in the middle of a rainstorm, water backs up or parts of your paths or driveway wash away.

Carrying a long-handled shovel, take a quick walk around your property. Make sure the ditches are clear; check the culvert entrances to make sure they haven't become blocked over the winter.

FIGURE 1.9 *Culverts under driveway*

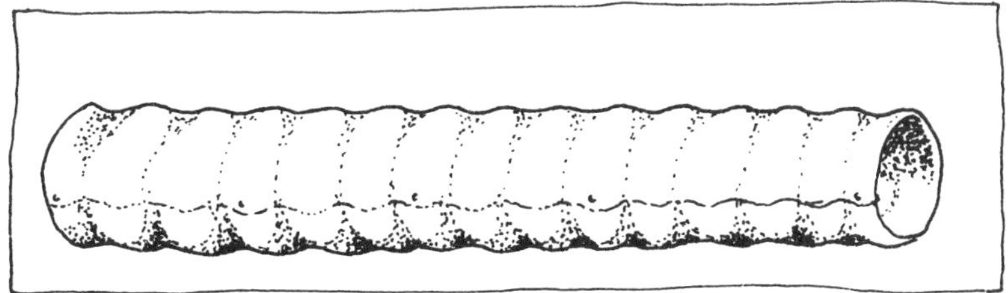

FIGURE 1.10 *Length of metal culvert*

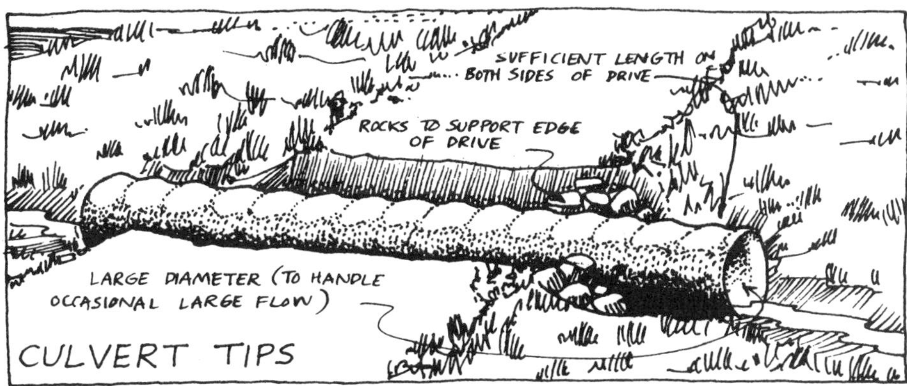

FIGURE 1.11 *Where to add a culvert*

FIGURE 1.12 *Culvert installation tips*

Poke around inside the culverts with the shovel from time to time. They are made to last a long time, but they can eventually rust out. It's far better to schedule replacement to suit your timetable rather than to have your driveway suddenly collapse because a culvert has given way.

A word of caution about culverts: the commonest mistake is to install a culvert that's too small. Choose one big enough to handle the maximum flow of water, even if such a rain occurs only once in every five years. If you don't, an unexpected torrential downpour could destroy the driveway, costing you much more than the price of a larger culvert.

DRIVEWAYS, PATHS, AND PARKING AREAS

Time was when most houses were approached on foot up the garden path and entered through the front door; the horse or carriage presumably was left by the front gate. The advent of automobiles and busier roads has left the front doors of many older houses high and dry, blindly facing a busy highway on which it is no longer safe for horse or automobile to tarry. Many of these older houses are now entered by what was once the back or side door, and a new approach has been necessarily created, often involving some form of driveway and parking space. Modern houses are designed with their main entrance oriented to the automobile's requirements, usually up a private driveway. In the suburbs, it may be a short suburban tarred strip; in the country, a longer shaled driveway leading to the house.

Whether you have a short or a long driveway, it will need certain maintenance from time to time. Make your inspection after you are sure the last snow has come and gone. If yours is a gravel driveway, clean up and rake back any gravel that may have been snowplowed off (usually onto the adjoining lawn).

If you have a blacktop driveway, check for cracks and holes. If these are minor, they can easily be repaired with special tars available from hardware stores and lumberyards. Occasionally, the whole driveway can benefit from a coat of blacktop sealer that creates a new wearing surface.

Similarly, minor repairs to concrete driveways are easily made at

FIGURE 1.13 *Blacktop sealer*

this stage using a concrete mix that can be bought in small sacks from building suppliers, lumberyards, and many hardware stores. (See pages 21–24 for more information on concrete repair.)

If yours is a longer driveway made of shale, crushed stone, split rock, or gravel, it will probably require more regular maintenance than either blacktop or concrete. Snowplowing, if necessary in your area, can exact a heavy toll by removing surface material along with the snow.

Any hole or rut—even a small one—will be enlarged by the action of rain and runoff and eventually become a major hazard. No matter how carefully a graded driveway is originally graded, sooner or later it will develop ridges and depressions that begin to collect water. The holes seem to grow of their own accord; in attempting to skirt them, drivers gradually change a smooth, straight run into a winding obstacle course.

This process, however, can be slowed greatly by a little rake-work now and then. When all the frost is out of the ground and any heaved sections have subsided—and the ground is reasonably dry—fill in holes and depressions with material raked from the high spots. If permanent ruts across the driveway persist from heavy rains and runoff, consider installing new or additional culverts to carry off the excess water.

Even though it is important not to begin to level your driveway or parking area until you are certain that cold weather has subsided and all the frost is gone, early spring is the best time of year to do this kind

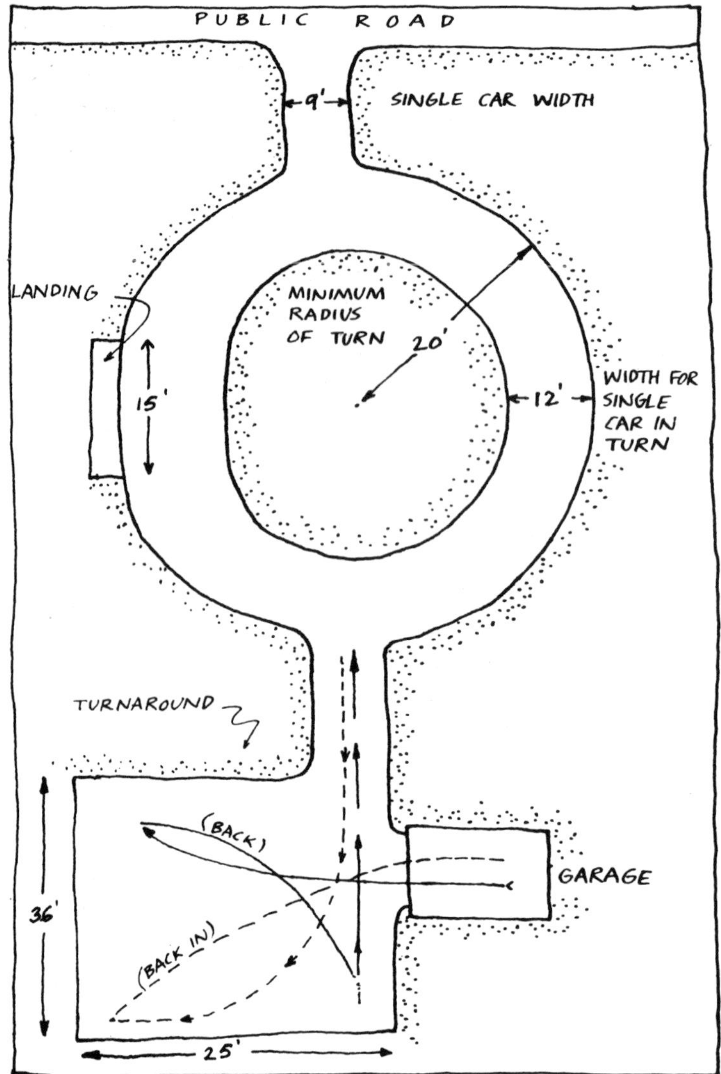

FIGURE 1.14 *Driveway dimensions*

of work, especially if you are undertaking more extensive repairs like major reshaling or adding additional parking space. Spring repairs allow the driveway to be compacted firmly (by use) during the summer, minimizing the amount of loose surface material that snowplows may later scrape away.

Much of what has been said about driveways is pertinent to paths. Paths and walkways that are not well drained or that are constructed over bases unsuited to their climate can suffer considerable damage—raised paving material, loosened bricks, and misplaced flagstones. Before attempting any repair, wait for the effects of winter or the rainy season to subside.

TERRACES AND PATIOS

Terraces and other outside paved areas such as patios and arbors should be inspected. Many are quite informal constructions—perhaps a few flagstones laid directly on the ground—and all that needs to be done is to make sure that no frost action has heaved them too severely out of position. If they have become too uneven, simply lift them up and move them aside (using a pickax is usually the easiest method) and use a spade to relevel the ground they rest on.

For larger, more formal areas, sometimes simple releveling of individual stones, bricks, tiles, or whatever is not sufficient; the whole area needs to be relaid. This can be a major project, since it may involve extensive excavating, installing beds of gravel for proper drainage and concrete walls for edge containment, and leveling sand in which the surface material should be laid.

If grass or other vegetation growing between the cracks is objectionable, consider installing a layer of black plastic immediately below the surface material rather than applying insecticide. An alternative method, more in harmony with the natural course of events, is to establish moss between the cracks.

GARDEN AND GROUNDS

If driveway repair, construction, or reconstruction has scarred your landscaping, reseed in the spring when growth is fastest. Ground broken in the fall is likely to remain a barren eyesore over the winter, leaching out valuable minerals and becoming subject to erosion.

As well as checking the driveway, paths, and walks around the house, cast an eye over the rest of your property. Has there been any damage from falling limbs or even fallen trees? Are all fences and walls still in good repair? Is your mailbox still standing securely? Has there been any damage to the shrubbery caused by heavy snows or any erosion caused by heavy rains? Spring is a good time to plan major landscaping work or other outdoor building—it is easier to accomplish before the growth of summer obscures the area and makes work too difficult.

Pruning of dead material is best done in spring. Since trees tend to grow rather large, any ornamentals near the house or walkways should be attended to on a regular basis by an insured professional. Spraying of any kind is to be discouraged, however, except in cases of extreme urgency. There are very few species-specific sprays, and if you use even the most benign insecticides or bactericides (such as B.T., a substance routinely recommended for pests such as gypsy moths) you usually kill off more than your intended victim—not to mention possibly infringing on your neighbors' rights not to be sprayed. By spraying for gypsy moth, for example, you kill not only the gypsy moth caterpillars but also the larval stages of practically all other species—most of which are essential for a balanced and healthy environment—that provide food for higher orders, the elimination of which inevitably reduces the bird population, and so on.

OUTSIDE UTILITIES

Many houses have their own supplies of cooking and heating gas, fuel oil, and sometimes large water-supply tanks installed on the property near the house. It is a good idea at this time of year to check the installation of such tanks to determine whether cold weather has caused them to shift in position, which could eventually result in a ruptured supply line. If frost or ground-heaving has been severe, it may be advisable to reposition the tanks more securely, but wait until all the frost and dampness are out of the ground and the tanks are as empty as possible. (For more information about tank maintenance, see pages 136–38.)

TWO

Structural Checkups

The period from spring through early summer is the ideal time to perform an annual inspection of the basic structure of your house. By keeping a regular eye on its exterior and interior framework, you'll be able to keep day-to-day running expenses—such as electricity and heating bills—to a minimum, as well as forestall major repair bills.

For convenience, this chapter is divided into two parts—as should be your inspection. The first part deals with what you can see from the outside; the second part, with what you can see from the inside.

THE EXTERIOR

The Walls

On a nice spring day, walk completely around the outside of your house, inspecting the condition of its external covering—referred to as the siding. The siding may all be one material, or it may combine materials, each of which can have its own set of problems. Aside from brick, other forms of masonry, and stucco (discussed a little later in this chapter), three types of material are used for siding: metal, painted or unpainted wood (other than wooden shingles), and shingles of various compositions.

METAL. The only metal commonly used for extensive exterior covering is aluminum. For this application, it usually comes as prefinished lengths, which resemble clapboards. As a result, it needs little attention; indeed, this is one of the few points in its favor. However, scratches and dents do occur. If you have to paint, use a paint made expressly for metal surfaces. Unpainted aluminum surfaces take paint better if they are first allowed to weather for a while and then given an undercoat of zinc-chromate metal primer. For unpainted areas of aluminum trim, such as window frames, a periodic coating of liquid wax will help prevent the pitting and discoloration that can occur under certain atmospheric conditions.

Apart from the actual siding, other metallic elements that may be visible on the outside of your house should be given some attention. Any iron or steel items such as bolt heads and various pieces of exterior hardware like shutter hinges and tension bolts should be kept painted or they will eventually rust away and leave stains running down the side of the building. Any exterior unpainted stainless steel or aluminum areas require only an occasional washing with soap and water to keep them clean and looking new; a light coat of paste wax will help protect them. Copper, brass, and bronze must all be kept polished if you want them to remain shiny. Copper roofs and flashing, though, are usually left to tarnish and develop a prestigious antique green patina.

WOOD. Wood is the commonest material used for the exterior covering of houses in the United States. Wood can be left untreated to weather, or it can be treated with various finishes—clear preservatives, stains, and paints. Wood siding ranges from rough-cut slab wood to decoratively milled and painted boards. The general types are as follows:

1. The first cut made from a log at a sawmill usually contains some bark edging. These boards are an attractive rustic design element when used as siding: although the boards are flat, the edges are irregular.
2. Rough-cut lumber used vertically, the joints covered with thin strips, is known as board and batten. It is usually stained or left

unpainted. Make sure that the battens remain in place, but take care that only one side of the vertical boards receives nails. If both sides are nailed, there is a danger of the board splitting. Nail the battens through the joints or only to that side of one of the boards it is covering that is already nailed.

3. Plain boards nailed horizontally, so that the bottom of one board overlaps the top of the board below, is known as weatherboarding. Usually made with rough-cut lumber, this type of wood siding requires attention mainly around framed openings where the excessive depth of two layers of boarding can present gaps that ought to be caulked.
4. Clapboarding overcomes this problem since the horizontal boards are thinner at their top edge than at their bottom edge, resulting in a thinner profile at these critical points. Clapboarding may be made of wood that is best left untreated—such as cedar or redwood—or from a type that is best protected by sealant or paint.
5. One form of horizontal wood siding lies flat by virtue of a rebate cut (large notch) in the bottom inside edge, which also eliminates any exposed joint and is therefore a better insulator. This siding is made in innumerable patterns, of which perhaps the so-called novelty siding is the commonest and best known.
6. A more modern variety of wood siding is composed of sheet plywood made usually to look like individual vertical boards. Although undeniably quicker to install, in the long run this is less economical since its lifespan is shorter and its repair costlier. Delamination and the need for regular surface treatment are shortcomings that must be accepted, along with the siding's questionable aesthetic value.

Whatever siding you have on your house, your first job is to look for damage to the wood itself, not to the finish. A beautifully painted piece of rotten wood is still a piece of rotten wood.

First, check places where the wood comes into contact with concrete or cement, such as around steps and porches. The design of such connections should force water to drain *away* from the wood, not toward it. Otherwise, the wood will eventually rot. Check places where wood might come into contact with the ground. An open invitation to termites, this situation should be corrected if you find it. A common error is to locate wood planter boxes against the foundation and siding, with no ventilation space between them and the house; this setup invites decay. Check the areas around gutters and downspouts to make sure that the siding is not subject to constant seepage from leaks or backups. Everything should drain away properly. Check the joints between the siding and all windows and doors to see whether all the seams are tightly caulked or filled (see pages 121–23 for adding or repairing caulking).

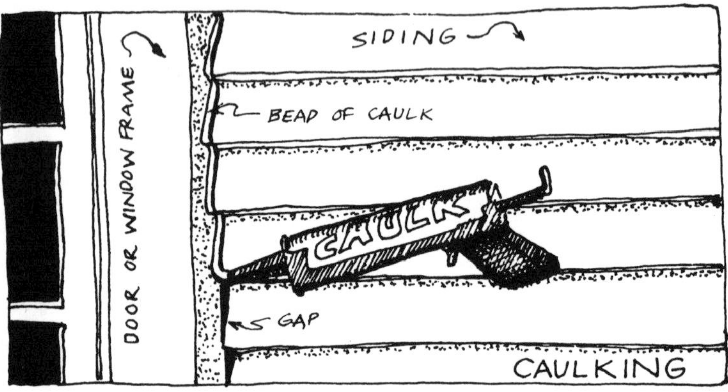

FIGURE 2.1 *Caulking joints between siding and windows*

If you find rot or decay at any of these points, the damaged wood must be removed and replaced. Products advertised as cures for rotted wood should be used sparingly—perhaps on one small section of a few square inches—and only when a more orthodox cure of complete replacement presents too great an expense. These products work by filling in the damaged area with a form of plastic and will not hold up over a wide expanse.

Perform these inspections on your siding once a year, and you will avoid expensive repairs. Your paint job (if the siding is painted) will last longer, too.

SHINGLES. If your house has wood or asbestos shingles, they should be inspected annually for splits, cracks, bulges, and missing pieces. Once this outer shingle covering is breached, water can easily reach

FIGURE 2.2 *Places to check for damaged wood siding*

the now-exposed sheathing and possibly the inner wall as well. If the shingles are misaligned or bulging, the nails holding them may simply have worked loose; all you have to do is to hammer them back in. If the nails no longer hold, hammer in new ones, but be sure to use galvanized, ringed nails (they grip well and do not rust). Drill a pilot hole first (to avoid splitting the shingle), and try to avoid hitting the shingle itself, for it tends to crack easily.

Cracked or split shingles need not be replaced. Slip a piece of waterproof building paper up behind the split and secure it with a galvanized nail through the butt (the lower or thicker end) of the shingle (again, drill a pilot hole first).

More seriously damaged shingles should be removed and replaced by new ones cut to the appropriate size. You may have to break up the damaged shingle even more, to get all the pieces out. You'll also have to take out, or cut out, the nails that were holding it in place, or you won't be able to insert the new shingle. As you're working on this, try not to damage adjoining shingles.

The nails holding asbestos shingles are generally visible and can be chiseled or sawn off or drilled out.

The nails holding wood shingles are usually applied through the top of the shingle and are consequently hidden by the shingle above. Although they are a little more difficult to remove, you can reach

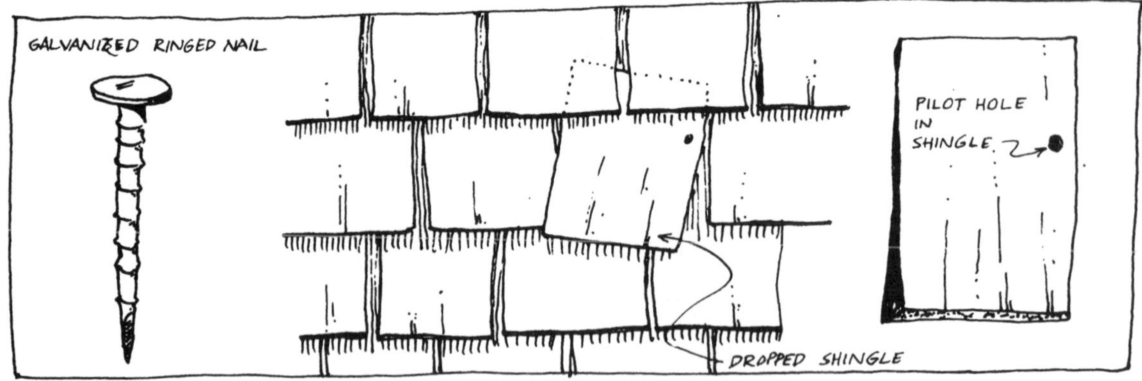

FIGURE 2.3 *Renailing loose shingles*

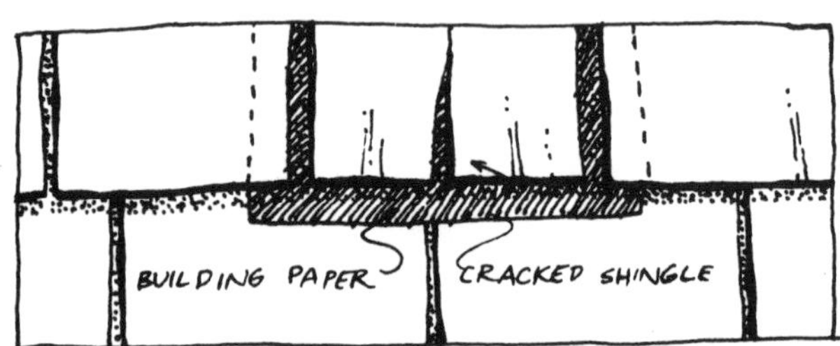

FIGURE 2.4 *Repairing a cracked shingle*

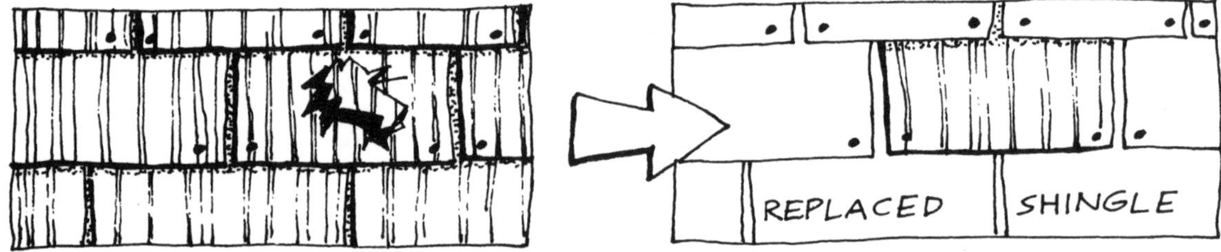

FIGURE 2.5 *Replacing a shingle*

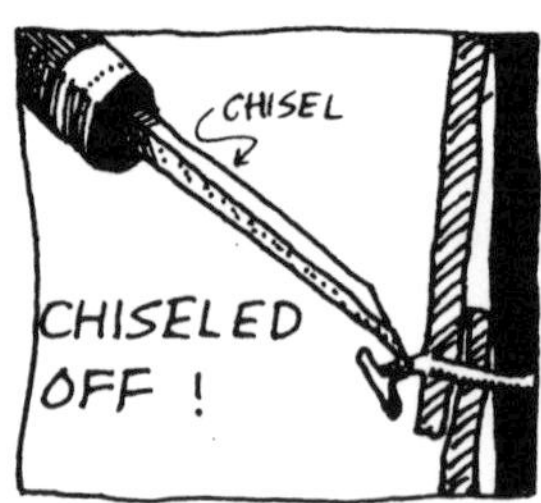

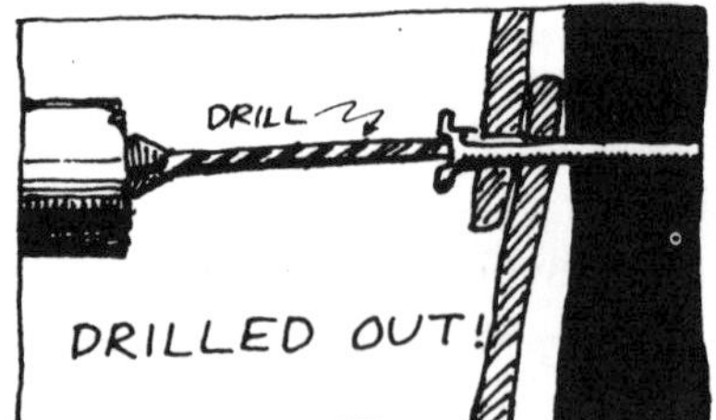

FIGURE 2.6 *Removing nails in asbestos shingles*

them by sliding a hacksaw blade up under the shingle to be removed and sawing through the shank of the nail. The head will then come out with the old shingle, leaving space to slide the new shingle into place. Nail the new shingle and all the adjoining ones through the butt ends.

Masonry

There is a surprising amount of masonry in the average home, even in a predominantly wood house. Its care and repair are the same no matter whether it is part of a concrete block or poured pier foundation, a walk or driveway, steps, patios, or brick, concrete block, or stuccoed walls.

Concrete is generally thought of as relatively indestructible, yet it can deteriorate seriously, even to the point of collapse. We're not talking about the violent damage caused by an earthquake; there are other forms of more insidious damage that can occur in the long run if concrete is left untreated. Settling foundations or excessive drying can cause minor cracks; in temperate regions the freeze-thaw-freeze cycle can enlarge these cracks to serious proportions. Rain or chronic dampness can also take their toll, resulting in conditions known by the ominous-sounding terms of *efflorescence* and *spalling*.

Extensive concrete deterioration should be attended to by a qualified engineer or builder, but small cracks and other minor damage can be repaired by the homeowner. The first time you make this annual home inspection, it would be helpful to list all the masonry parts in and around your house. Look for the following defects, some of which call for more immediate attention than others.

CRACKS. Small hairline cracks are almost unavoidable on large areas of masonry, such as a stuccoed wall or a smoothly cemented concrete walk. But if a crack is obviously too wide to be hidden by a coat of paint, you should easily be able to repair it.

The procedure is reasonably simple: start by undercutting the crack (see figure 2.8), then clean it out, wet it, and patch it. The purpose of the undercutting is to prevent the patch from falling out; this job is best done with a hardened-steel tool called a cold chisel.

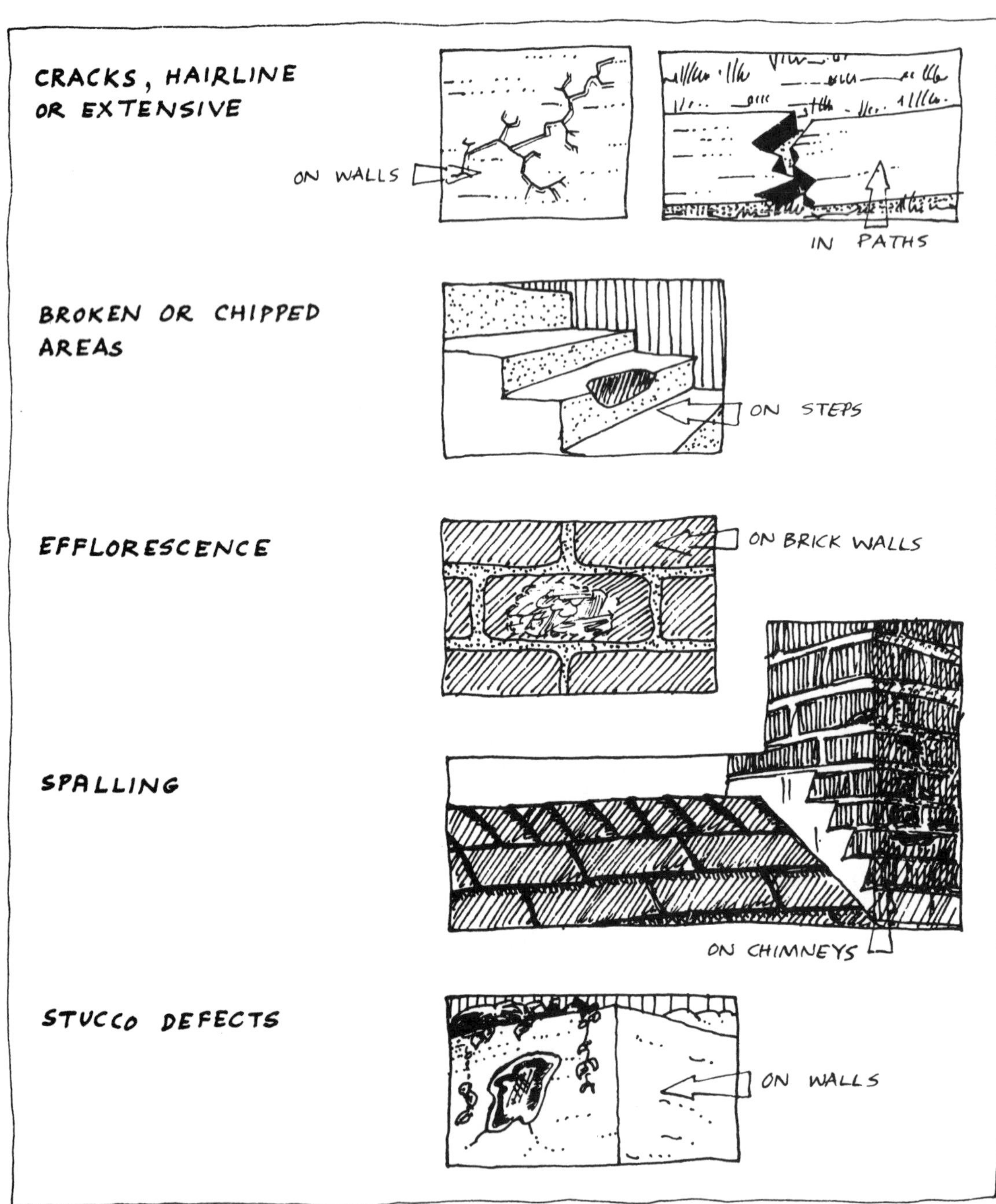

FIGURE 2.7 *Concrete defects (cracks, broken areas, efflorescence, spalling, stucco defects)*

Cleaning out is easiest with a stiff wire brush; removing all loose particles ensures a good bond. Wetting down any areas that will be in contact with new cement prevents the old concrete from drawing moisture from the new before it has had time to cure (set) properly. Don't leave so much water, however, that it dilutes the new concrete. As a further guarantee of a good bond between the old and new work, apply a latex bonding agent—there are various brands available, all with slightly different application procedures clearly indicated on the containers—to the existing surface of the area to be repaired.

Finally, fill the crack. You can use cement you've mixed yourself—one part Portland cement to three parts sand. The mix shouldn't be sloppy (too much water) or very stiff (too little). A mason's adage goes: If you can throw the mix against a wall and have it stick, it's just right. You can make life easier by using premixed material that comes in bags from 10 pounds to 90 pounds. Follow the instructions on the bag. For small jobs you can buy patching material—latex, epoxy, vinyl, acrylic cement—in cartridge form.

Using a trowel (figure 2.10), work the material well into the crack, removing all air bubbles. After smoothing the patch, keep it damp by covering it with plastic and wetting it down occasionally for the first 48 hours. If it dries too quickly, it will crack again and you'll be back where you started.

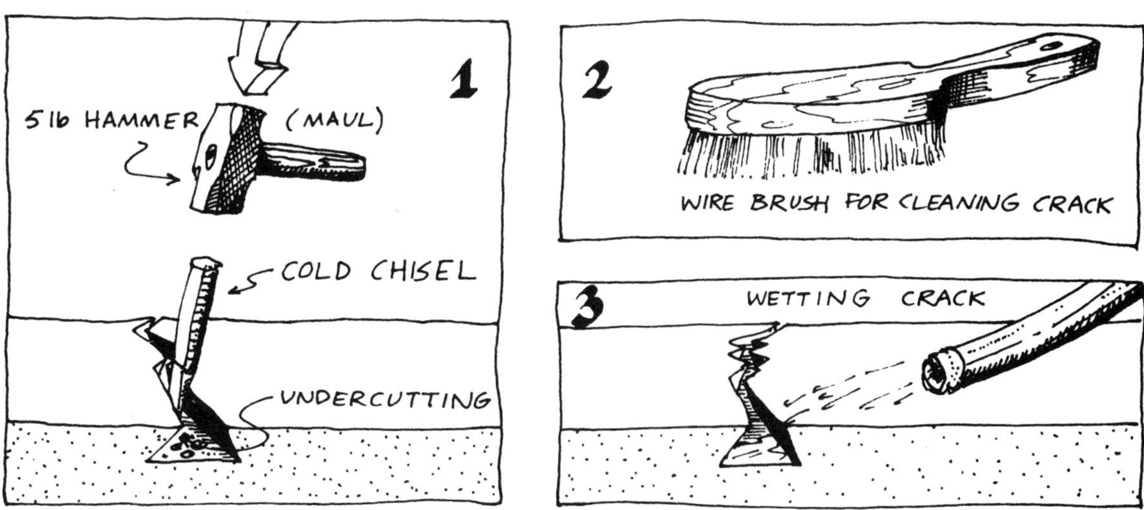

FIGURE 2.8 *Preparing a crack for repair*

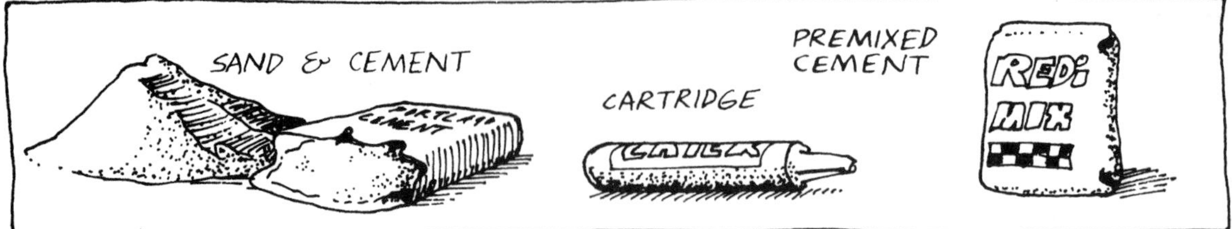

FIGURE 2.9 *Repair materials*

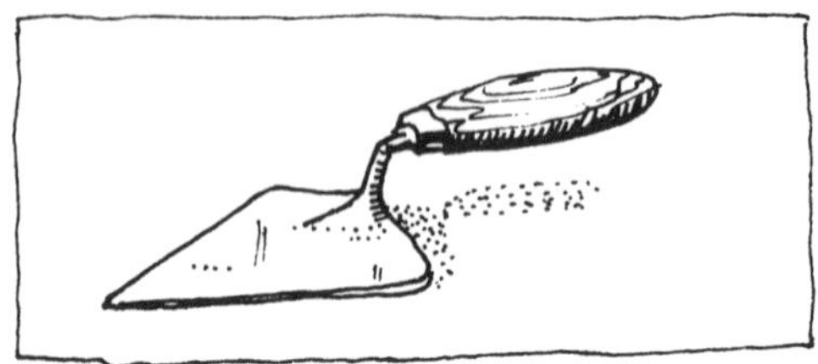

FIGURE 2.10 *Trowel*

Use the same basic procedure even if the crack is wide, deep, or has uneven sides. With flat surfaces, such as paths and walkways, however, it's a good idea to try to elevate a sunken side and keep it level by packing sand underneath.

Whenever severe cracks have caused the surface to become very uneven, you must first find out the cause of the problem and correct it before repairing the surface. Poor drainage is often the culprit. Concrete walkways, for example, can deteriorate rapidly if not properly drained or if the foundation is inadequate in a region where there is freezing weather. If the problem is ground subsidence or fault-related earth movements (more common in certain sections of the United States), however, there is little that can be done.

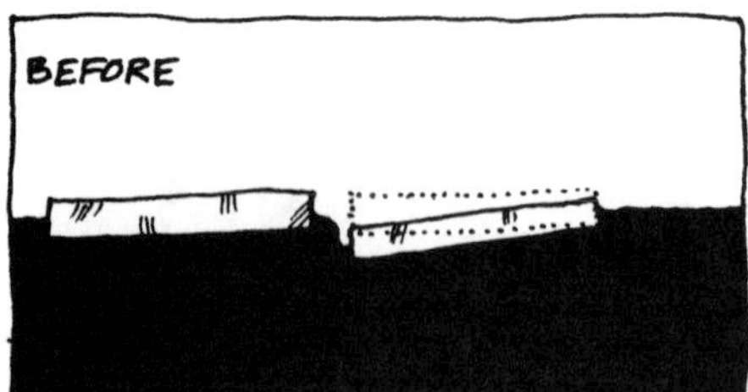

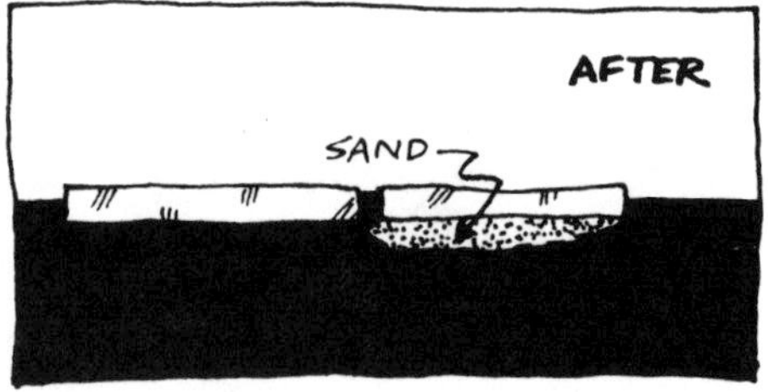

FIGURE 2.11 *Leveling paving stones*

BROKEN CONCRETE. The procedure for repairing larger holes and broken-out areas, such as the edge of a concrete step, is similar to the process of repairing cracks, with one addition. Start by providing a proper base for the patching material—chip away a flat space with a cold chisel (see figure 2.12). Now you have to build up some front support for the wet mix (this is the additional step). Grease the support so that concrete will not stick to it when it is removed, and fix it firmly in place, because wet concrete is very heavy.

The mix should contain some gravel or small stones (that's the ingredient that turns cement into concrete). Just as when repairing a crack, it is of paramount importance to allow the repair to cure slowly by keeping it damp and covered to start with. Depending on the weather and the thickness of the new work, it can take up to a week to harden completely. If there's any doubt, give it longer.

FIGURE 2.12 ***Repairing steps***

EFFLORESCENCE. Sometimes mineral salts contained in bricks, especially new bricks, are pushed to the surface by moisture. The often unsightly result is known as efflorescence. It can be removed by a rigorous cleaning of the bricks with a wire brush and a solution consisting of one part muriatic acid and four parts water. Muriatic acid is strong, and very dangerous if handled carelessly, so follow the directions on the container with care. Continued efflorescence is best cured by eliminating the source of the moisture. Refer to the sections on tracing and eliminating roof leaks, maintaining gutters and downspouts, and ensuring that exterior openings are properly caulked—all of which can be potential causes of continued efflorescence.

SPALLING. This unusual term comes from an old Scottish word used in quarries and stoneyards: *spale,* meaning "chip" or "splinter." Spalling is the process of deterioration caused by brickwork's soaking up moisture and then flaking apart during freezing weather as the moisture becomes ice and expands. Badly spalled bricks should be removed and replaced (see figure 2.13). The replacement bricks can be treated with a clear brick-sealant to prevent a recurrence of the condition. (Mortar, which is cement with added lime, may, like patching cement, be bought in small ready-mixed quantities.)

STUCCO DEFECTS. Stucco, which actually means any kind of plasterwork, usually refers to an outer covering of cement. Sometimes the stucco on exterior walls is *pebbledash*—a mixture of cement and fine stones. A mortar pigment is often added to color the stucco. Repairing cracks or holes in colored stucco can be difficult, because it is almost impossible to match the original color. To achieve uniformity, you may have to give the whole surface a new finish coat.

Cracks in stucco are repaired like cracks in concrete: chip away

FIGURE 2.13 *Replacing bricks*

and undercut, clean out the crack, wet the area, and apply a finish coat. For actual holes, the repair should be done in three stages, as the original stucco was put on. The first coat, called the *scratch coat,* is applied over chicken wire—if the area is badly damaged, you may have to repair the wire as well—and allowed to dry for 48 hours. Before it dries completely, however, scratch the surface to provide for better adhesion of the second coat—hence the name scratch coat. The second coat should be allowed to dry for up to four days before applying the finish coat.

FIGURE 2.14 ***Stucco repair***

The Roof

Normally, a roof should not need an annual inspection—asphalt shingles can be expected to last for 15 years at least, cedar shakes for 20, and slate, tile, and tin roofs for much, much longer.

Since one of the main functions of the roof is to keep the house dry, any sign of water inside means that something is wrong. The first step to take is a quick visual check of the roof covering. See if any part of it has blown away, if branches of overhanging trees have fallen and caused any damage, or if any flashing seems to be damaged. (The flashing is the metal strip covering the seams where chimneys emerge, or abut the roof, or at the inside junction of different roof slopes, called *valleys.*)

When you're trying to spot the reason for a leak, remember that a leak inside the house may have traveled some distance down a rafter

FIGURE 2.15
Problems to look for on the roof

or across a beam before appearing on the ceiling, so don't confine your search to the area immediately above its appearance on the inside.

ROOF COVERINGS. Even if you have no leaks now, keeping an eye on the condition of the roof covering can help avoid them in the future. If you have an asphalt-shingle roof, the shingles should not be flaking, cracked, or excessively curled. They should still show a good covering of surface granules; if they are bald or shiny in spots, it's time to think about replacing them.

Wood shingles, regardless of their type, should not be eaten away at the edges or cracked. A certain amount of mossy growth is not necessarily bad, but if the wood has been chemically treated (for increased longevity and fire retardancy), it's an indication that the treatment may be losing its potency.

Perhaps the most important thing you can do to maintain a roof is to ensure that it is clean and is draining well. This entails cleaning away any debris (fallen leaves and pine needles are the worst offenders) from corners or valleys and making sure the runoff system (gutters and downspouts) is in top working order.

GUTTERS AND DOWNSPOUTS. One reason for inspecting the roof at this time of year is that winter snow and ice may have been hard on the runoff system. If gutters have been damaged by heavy snow loads, and downspouts disconnected or clogged, heavy spring rains can impair the general drainage situation around the house and contribute to basement leaks.

Gutters are designed to collect the rain that falls on the roof and conduct it away from the house safely. The rainwater can even be directed into a rain barrel or storage tank for use during dry times (it may well be softer than your tap water). However, don't use rainwater collected from a roof newly reshingled with asphalt shingles (especially in areas of the United States where shingles made with asbestos ingredients are still permitted); it may be full of the surfacing granules, some of which wash off at first. Similarly, do not drink rainwater collected from a wood roof treated with (possibly toxic) fire preventative or wood preservative.

The damage from an impaired runoff system to plants is obvious—they will be washed away.

The damage to a foundation from an impaired gutter system is subtle but can result in serious problems that require a draconian cure, such as massive excavation to repair foundation walls and drainage systems. Of course, when it was built, the house should have been sited so that water drains away from it. This ensures a dry basement and a firm foundation. A properly working gutter-and-

FIGURE 2.16 *Damage to foundation plantings*

downspout system contributes to this. But by allowing rain to run off the roof all around the house, an impaired system actually fills the area next to the foundation full of water. In freezing weather, all this excess water in the ground can become a powerful force if it turns to ice, putting enormous pressure against the foundation.

Each house's roof design dictates the gutter layout, but the essentials always remain the same: Provide gutters large enough to contain the rain from the area served; provide sufficient slope to the gutters to avoid standing water, which will rust out or, in the case of wood gutters, rot out the gutters; and ensure that you have adequate and efficient downspouts to lead the water away from the house (or into a collecting receptacle such as a storage tank or rain barrel).

The first thing to check is that the whole system is connected—lengths may have become separated and downspouts may have broken loose.

Second, make sure that there are no obstructions—matted leaves, twigs, and so forth—in the gutters, or blockages in the downspouts.

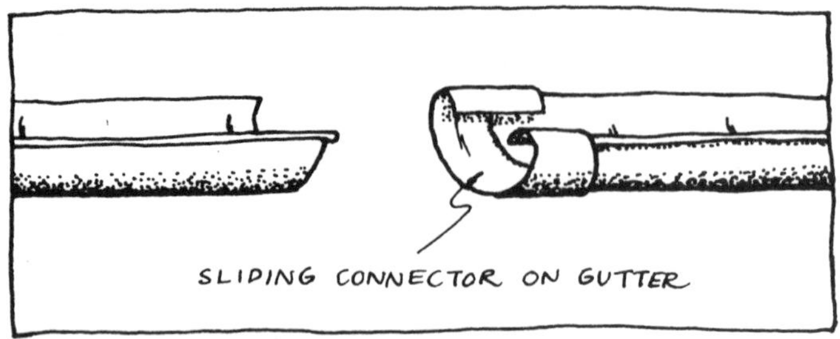

FIGURE 2.17
Gutter and downspout connections

The gutter entrance to a downspout is usually protected by a wire basket or strainer designed to prevent leaves and other debris from washing into the downspout. These containers often act as effective starting points for leaf dams, however, and must be cleaned regularly. Moreover, they can eventually rust or distort, in which case they should be replaced. Use only similar metals—that is, aluminum strainers for aluminum gutters, copper with copper, and so on.

One way to check the free flow in downspouts is to take a hose up to the top and run a strong stream of water through, taking care that an obstruction doesn't cause the water to splash back at you and that the outflow is safely conducted away without eroding the area at the bottom of the pipe.

Third, check that the gutters are sloped correctly and sufficiently; a ½-inch fall for every 8 feet of length is generally enough. If they are improperly positioned, you may have to readjust some of the gutter supports or hangers. This generally entails no more than prying out or unscrewing existing supports, but if the roofline is high it may be best to employ professionals to undertake the job. Note that very long runs of gutter sometimes drain at both ends and consequently slope two ways.

Finally, check that there are no holes in the system caused by standing water that rusted out a section. If the system is still basically intact, but shows signs of rust, scrape away the rust and paint the gutters, inside and out, with special rustproofing paint. This is much easier and cheaper than ignoring the rust and eventually having to replace the entire system.

FIGURE 2.18 *Leaf dams*

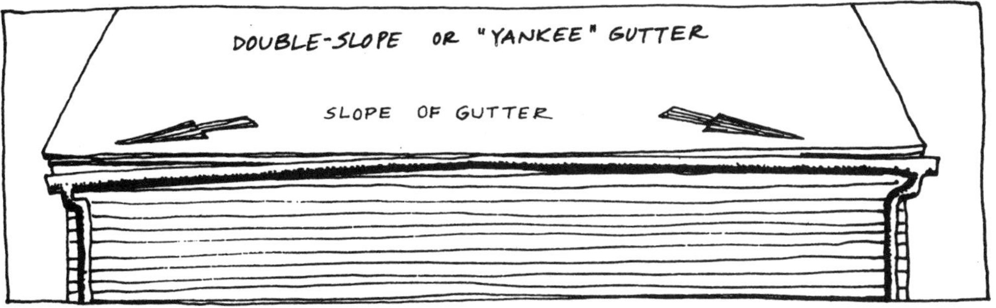

FIGURE 2.19 *Double-sloping gutter*

Houses with wood gutters, or gutters that are built into the eaves, ought to be inspected more assiduously than houses with attached metal gutters, since repair or replacement of these types is more expensive.

FIGURE 2.20 *Wooden gutters and eave gutters*

THE INTERIOR

Foundations and Basements

In most sections of the United States, below-grade foundations are necessary so that the houses can be supported below the level at which the ground may freeze. With such construction, you can see more of the foundation from the inside than from the outside.

In warmer parts of the country, however, foundation systems may be entirely visible from the outside. Such houses—the foundation consists of wood, metal, or concrete piers—do not have a basement or cellar. Nevertheless, the area immediately below the floor (called the *crawl space*) should still be inspected from time to time. Even if it appears completely closed off, and no matter how shallow it may be, there is usually some access, either a small door or removable panel. Open this and look inside from time to time. What you should look for is detailed below in the discussion of full basements.

Even if your cellar or basement is never used, it must be inspected periodically. A lot of serious—and expensive—trouble can start here. The three main enemies in this area are masonry deterioration, wood rot and decay, and insect damage. Additional problems include excess water and the presence of radon gas.

VENTS. When winter is past and the weather warms up, you should open the basement vents, if you have them. These vents, which should have been closed at the beginning of winter (see chapter 8), are one of the keys to keeping the basement or crawl space dry and well ventilated. The general rule for providing sufficient ventilation is one vent in each corner, or one vent for every 8 feet of perimeter, whichever is less.

A basement equipped with windows is likely to be a more substantial area than one equipped only with vents, and as such should not need more ventilation than any other similar area in the house receives in the normal course of events.

FIGURE 2.21 *Typical basement vent*

MASONRY INSPECTION. Most houses have some form of masonry foundation—brick, stone, concrete, or concrete block. Properly built masonry constructions are generally long-lasting, but they *can* fail and you should know what to look for.

A little crumbling mortar and a few cracks, if not extensive, can be repaired by patching or filling (see pages 21–24). They present no major problem. In fact, if the house is old, some such deterioration can be expected. But if all the mortar joints are soft or powdery to the touch, you may be accumulating too much water on the outside of the foundation wall (see chapter 1). On the other hand, the condition may result from too much dampness inside the basement. If the former is the problem, it should be obvious from pools of standing water or other consequences of poor drainage mentioned earlier. If the latter is the problem, you will know by the indications suggested in chapter 9 under the discussion of "Humidity," where you will also find remedies. In either case, once the cause has been eliminated, the joints should be cleaned out and recemented—a process known as *pointing*.

Pointing may be done simply by first chipping out the old loose mortar, wetting the joint, and applying fresh mortar with a small trowel. (Whenever you do any chipping of masonry, wear some form of eye protection.) Use a narrow, cold chisel to remove the old mortar to a depth of no more than ½ inch. Work carefully; you do not want to damage the bricks themselves. Use a stiff brush to remove loose particles from the surface of the remaining mortar before wetting the surface.

There are special pointing tools for pushing the mortar into the joint, but any firm substitute will work as well, provided you avoid leaving any air pockets. Fill the vertical joints first, then fill the horizontal joints continuously across the entire width being pointed. Try to avoid getting mortar on the face of the brick. Finally, clean the surface and strike the joints to match the existing joints.

Small cracks, especially hairline cracks in poured concrete, have little effect on the overall structure, but larger, extensive cracks that you can slip your little finger into can presage a bigger problem, such as settling or excessive pressure on the outside of the foundation wall.

These situations should be repaired as soon as possible for they represent a real structural hazard; they also open the way, literally, to water seepage and insect penetration. Sometimes all that is required is better drainage outside and some minor masonry repair inside. In other cases, especially if the ground has settled, it may be necessary to jack up that part of the house and replace the weakened section of foundation. This is a job for professionals and can become progressively more expensive the longer it is left, so catch it early by

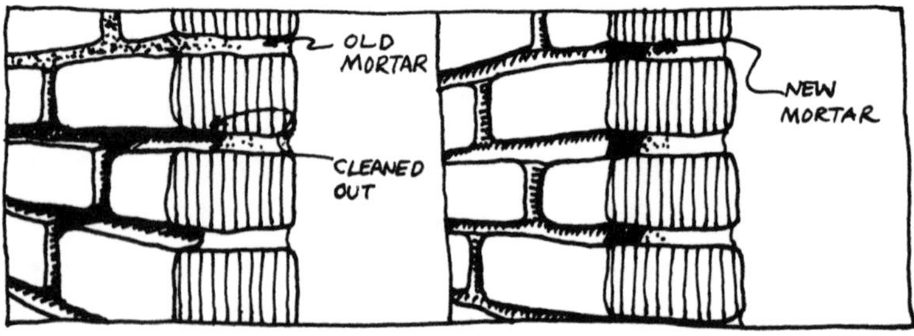

FIGURE 2.22 *Pointing*

regular inspection at this time of the year. If you have any doubts, get a professional opinion as soon as you can.

The perimeter walls are the most important, but check all parts of the foundation, including piers and interior walls, for cracks, settling, and deterioration.

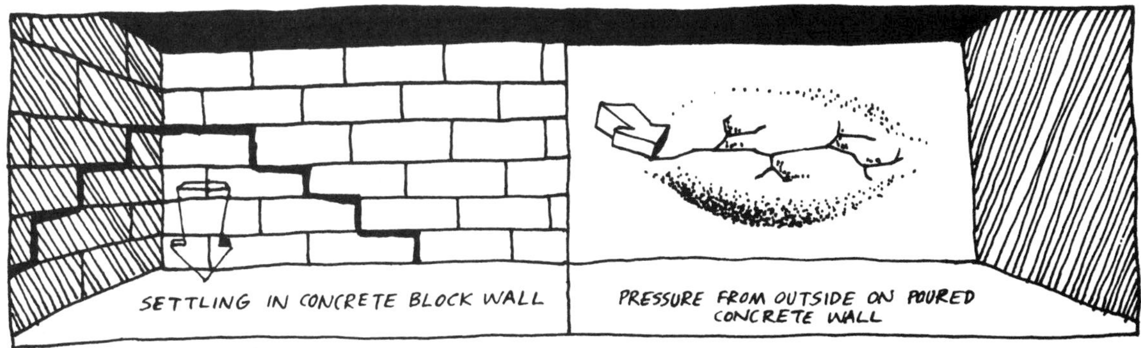

FIGURE 2.23 *Serious cracks*

FIGURE 2.24 *Piers*

WOOD DETERIORATION. Rot or decay—even so-called dry rot—is caused by tiny plants called fungi, which can live only in wood with a moisture content of at least 30 percent (and the warmer it is, the faster they grow). This is yet another reason for controlling the humidity in your house, especially in the basement (see chapter 9).

Check all the structural wood in the basement for rot both by visual inspection—look for soft, wet areas and parts covered with fungus—and, since rot is not always evident on the surface, by probing with a sharp knife or other pointed instrument. If the wood is hard and resists the probe, it is sound, but if it feels soft and mushy inside, decay is present.

Any sign of rot is serious because it can spread and severely weaken the wood. Unless there is a simple, obvious solution to the moisture problem, and you can support the rotted section easily, ask a professional's opinion. Large sections of damaged wood may have to be removed and replaced with sound wood, preferably treated with preservative. You must also ensure that the cause is completely eliminated. This is not a job for the ordinary homeowner.

A few words about preservatives: all are toxic and some are carcinogenic. They give off harmful vapors and should not be used indoors. If wood is to be in contact with the ground, a preservative will be effective only if it has been applied under pressure. Soaking wood in preservative provides less protection in such a situation and simply painting it on provides even less. Preservatives can also cause subsequent coats of paint to peel. The best way to preserve wood is to keep it dry and out of contact with the ground. If you feel compelled to use a chemical preservative, exercise extreme caution. Read the labels thoroughly and follow safety instructions. Many areas now prohibit the use of some of these products.

FIGURE 2.25 *Three common wood preservatives*

INSECTS. Certain insects can seriously damage houses, among them wood-destroying beetles, carpenter ants, and termites. By far the most dangerous are termites, since their presence is often the least obvious. Termites, which feed on the wood from the inside, can sometimes be detected on sunny spring days when they swarm. They can be identified by their two pairs of long wings of equal size—

unlike carpenter ants, whose two pairs of wings are of unequal size. The difference is also seen in the termite's thick waist versus the ant's slender waist.

Termites betray their presence even if you don't see them swarm. You may find discarded wings underneath doors and windows and light fixtures, to which they are attracted when swarming. Even more

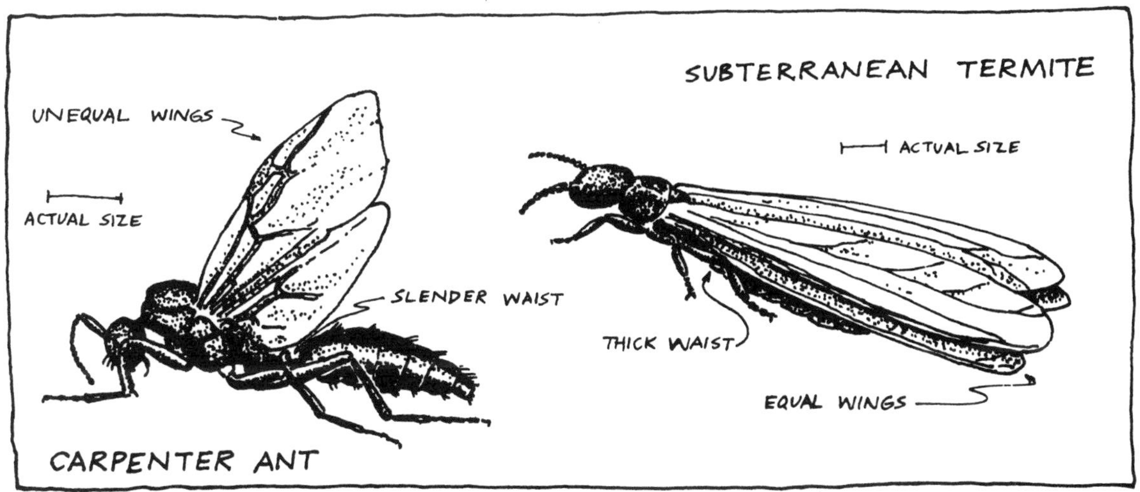

FIGURE 2.26 *Ants and termites*

revealing are their characteristic shelter tubes. These are little tubes of earth, which can be seen on masonry walls, enabling the termites to travel from the earth to the wood without exposing themselves.

Carpenter ants can be detected by telltale piles of sawdust. Unlike termites, which eat the wood, carpenter ants merely excavate it for living quarters, but the result is the same—honeycombed wood, disastrously weakened from within. The ants also are more visible, since they do not build tubes. Prevention is the best remedy. Keep the basement dry and well ventilated; avoid putting near the house piles of rotting wood in which the ants can nest; and inspect regularly. If you do discover ants just patiently follow them until you find the nest (usually outside somewhere) and then destroy it and seal the entrance they have been using to the house—typically around porches, steps, and where the wood meets the foundation. Again, any damaged wood may have to replaced, depending on the extent of loss.

Beetles can be detected by small round or oval holes in the wood-

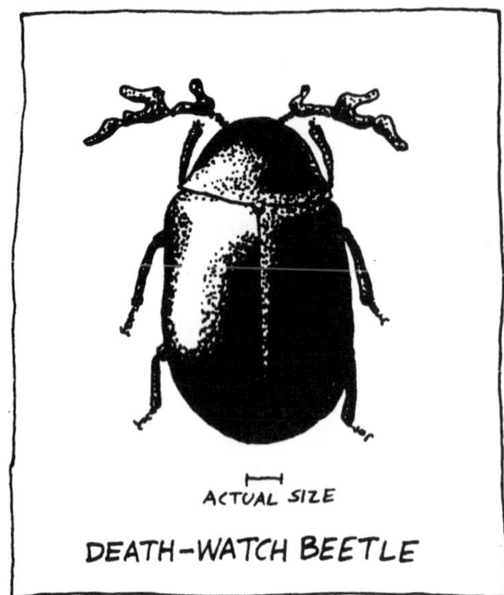

FIGURE 2.27 *Death-watch beetle*

work and powdery deposits around the holes. Beetles come and go, and since treatment is expensive, before you spend large sums of money, make an easy test to determine whether an infestation is still active. Wipe away the powdery deposits, and wait a few days to see if new powder, and holes, appear.

Against all these pests, the best defense is a dry, well-ventilated basement and a thorough inspection at least once a year. If you do find evidence of any of these insects, especially termites, don't panic. Over time these pests can cause a lot of damage, but it takes years for them to have any serious effects on a house.

Getting rid of an insect infestation permanently is a job for a professional who knows how to handle the strong and potentially dangerous chemicals that are used in such cases. How can you find a reputable inspection service that will not overtreat the problem and expose you and your family to needless toxic risk? For a start, ask experienced friends, real estate agents, or the local Better Business Bureau for referrals. As further insurance, call the county or state consumer fraud agency in your area to make sure there are no complaints filed against the inspection service in question. Discuss with the exterminator the kinds of chemicals to be used against termites and other pests and make sure that all appropriate cautions are taken to avoid accidental seepage of any of the chemicals into the living areas of your home.

WET BASEMENT. Over time, a wet basement can become much more than an annoyance. The moisture will turn the basement into a breeding ground for mold and mildew. It can rust tools and rot wood.

In extreme cases, the water will erode the house's foundation by leaching lime from the mortar joints.

If you have this problem, in whatever degree, first determine how the water gets in. You don't have to do much investigating if water pours in after a rainstorm. The cause of a dank and moldy basement isn't always that obvious, however. Water can be carried in with humid air that condenses when it hits the cold cellar walls, or it can seep through porous concrete and cracks. If you can't see where the dampness comes from, you can run a simple test to pinpoint its source. Wait until the affected wall is dry, then tape a piece of aluminum foil or a mirror tightly to it. When the dampness recurs, inspect the foil.

If the side of the foil facing you is wet, the problem is condensation. That can be reduced rather easily and cheaply. Here are some measures to try:

- Make sure your clothes dryer vents to the outside.
- Close basement doors and windows as tightly as possible during the summer to keep hot, humid air out of the basement. But open the doors and windows on cool, dry days to hasten evaporation.
- A dehumidifier can draw excess moisture out of the air day after day. If the other measures don't prove effective, this appliance may do the trick. (See Ratings of dehumidifiers in the appendix.)

If the side of the foil facing the wall is wet, water is coming through the basement walls from the outside. As excess water builds up in the ground surrounding the house, it presses against the basement walls. The pressure eventually forces the water through the walls at the points of least resistance—through gaps and cracks in the exterior waterproofing, then inside through the cracks, joints, and porous concrete or masonry.

There are no miracle cures for a wet basement, but the following measures can alleviate the problem:

1. Patch cracks. Cracks and holes can be filled with hydraulic cement, a quick-setting compound sold at paint and hardware

stores that expands when it contacts water. It can even be used to plug a hole while water is seeping through.

2. Paint over minor seepage. In some cases, two coats of basement waterproofing paint can eliminate the dampness caused by a minor amount of seepage or weeping (see Ratings of waterproofing paints in the appendix).
3. Divert the water from the outside. The more important measures (and usually the easier ones to handle) are designed to improve the grading and drainage around the house. For example, be sure that the ground slopes away from the house. Remove dense shrubbery that abuts the foundation wall. The soil under the shrubbery won't dry out if sunlight can't reach it. Keep gutters and downspouts clean and in good repair. If local building codes permit, direct the water from the downspouts to the storm sewer. Otherwise, channel the runoff away from the house or to a dry well.

   Below-ground window wells need a liner, plus a base of gravel, to ensure that water drains from the well properly. You can also buy plastic window-well covers to keep out rain and snow.
4. Make underground repairs. These are messy, potentially expensive remedies, best handled by a waterproofing contractor. The contractor may rip up all or part of the perimeter of the basement floor and install drain tiles. The tiles, actually perforated pipe, direct the water to a sump pump that pumps the water away from the base of the house.

Some houses may need better waterproofing and drainage on the outside. The contractor will excavate to expose the outside of the foundation walls, then apply new layers of waterproofing and set drain tiles at the footings.

If you do decide to use a contractor, get bids from at least three. When you settle on one and are ready to sign a contract, be sure you can withhold the final payment until after the work has been completed. That delay gives you time to be sure the work was done properly. It also gives the contractor an incentive to fix anything that wasn't done right the first time.

RADON. Radon is a colorless, odorless, radioactive gas formed wherever uranium is present in the earth's crust. The gas, like any radioactive element, spontaneously decays, producing particles that have been dubbed "radon daughters." Radon is an easily inhaled gas, and radon daughters are small enough to lodge deep in the lung. Don't ignore this recently documented hazard of twentieth-century life—as many as one in every 100 people may die of radon-induced lung cancer.

Radon, being a gas, quickly dissipates in the open air. But if it seeps into a house, it can collect in dangerous concentrations. Radon enters a house through holes and cracks in the foundation, through porous cinderblock, and around loose-fitting pipes, floor drains, or sump pumps. It collects in the highest concentrations in the areas closest to the earth—typically, the basement. Although radon-bearing air can diffuse through the house or travel through the heating or air-conditioning system, little is usually found above the second floor of a building.

Dangerous as it is, the radon problem is easy to solve. In most cases, homeowners who are living with dangerously high levels of radon can reduce it to acceptable levels for a few hundred dollars. The job rarely costs more than $1,500. Every home should be tested for radon, especially since there's no way to predict which house has radon and which does not. In some parts of the country, radon tests have joined termite inspections as routine conditions for a house sale.

The first step is to buy a detector. Many hardware stores and even some supermarkets sell them now. If you can't find one, call your state department of environmental protection. The agency can provide you with a list of radon-testing companies that have passed the EPA's Radon Measurement Proficiency program. Or you may be able to get a radon test free—some utility companies offer one as part of an energy audit.

There are two main types of test device: short-term devices, most commonly charcoal canisters; and longer-term testers, such as alpha-track detectors. The former provides a reading of the radon levels encountered in three to seven days; the latter provides an average reading of the exposure over a period of three months to one year. Both types cost about $25, including analysis by a lab and a report of the results. If your home has never been tested, it's best to start with a short-term device. Put it in the lowest part of the house—the basement or, if there's no basement, the first floor. Do the test at a time of year when you keep all the doors and windows closed. If the results come back less than 4 picoCuries (pCi/1) or so, you don't have an urgent radon problem.

Test a second time if the level is high. Radon levels can vary greatly over time. For the second test, use a longer-term detector and place it in the rooms where your family spends the most time. If the detector shows that the radon level over time is elevated, you need to take action. State environmental protection departments, as well as the EPA, can provide a list of approved contractors able to make radon-reducing modifications.

The main method used to reduce the radon level is to improve the ventilation where the radon concentrates. In some homes, the solution might be as simple as installing a fan in the basement. In colder climates, a heat-recovery ventilation system might be used. A very effective solution is what's called a "sub-slab suction system," in which two pipes hooked up to an outside fan pierce the concrete slab to the gravel below. A relatively small flow of air there can reduce radon levels dramatically. Other methods include sealing all possible entry points in the basement or providing a separate air source for furnaces, clothes dryers, wood stoves, and other devices that lower indoor air pressure by venting air to the outdoors. Lowering the indoor air pressure increases the flow of radon into the house from the underlying soil.

The Main Living Area

The second major inspection at this time is of the general condition of the structural fitted woodwork inside the house. This is often referred to collectively as the *millwork,* since many of the parts involved are often manufactured at the mill—rather than on the site as the house is being built. However, we've also included here a look at the cabinetry and hardware in the house.

FLOORS. After the heating system has been running for a while, some floor problems may become more evident. This is therefore a good time of year to assess common floor conditions, such as shrinking, swelling, squeaking, and sagging.

Shrinking. Gaps between floorboards, caused by the wood shrinking, are most likely to show up at this time of year, when the house is probably at its driest. The problem is most common with wider-board softwood floors, such as pine.

If the floor is new, the shrinkage probably reflects the wood's natural seasoning, which ideally should have been accomplished before it was laid. Otherwise, a seasonal shrinking (and subsequent swelling) indicates insufficient humidity control (see chapter 9). This seasonal movement can be reduced somewhat by sealing the wood with a surface or penetrating finish to make it more impervious to moisture. Penetrating finishes actually sink into the wood, sealing it. They usually go on in two coats. Surface finishes, such as paint, also effectively seal the wood. There are so many products available that it is difficult to generalize on application procedures, but it should be noted that not all are interchangeable or universally applicable over one another. Your floor, which may benefit from a sealing, may already have some kind of finish; it is important to identify this finish and read the indications on the proposed new sealer to make sure the two are compatible. If not, or if you are in any doubt, the best course is to remove the first finish.

If the floor is relatively old and there are gaps of up to ½ inch or more between boards, it is possible to fill these with wedge-shaped fillets of any available wood (though the same type and color are preferable). Make sure that the thick edge of the wedge is larger than the gap, pound the fillet in using a block of scrap wood (see figure 2.28), and then plane or sand the whole thing level.

Swelling. Swelling and buckling of floorboards are caused by a floor absorbing too much moisture—perhaps as a result of rain damage or a plumbing leak—and are more serious than shrinking.

You may be able to level the floor by drying the wood as much as possible first (use a heat lamp). Then try to flatten the boards either by nailing through them into the joist below or by screwing up through the subfloor from underneath to pull them down.

For more serious swelling that cannot be reduced enough by drying, you will have to remove a board and replace it with a narrower one. This occurs more frequently with narrow, tongue-and-groove flooring than with wide boards.

When a section of tongue-and-groove flooring has really buckled, especially the narrower, hardwood types, it shouldn't prove difficult to pull or pry one board loose. But try to avoid damaging the edges of the adjacent boards. If there is any danger of this, try splitting the board along its center with a chisel, and pry it free from this point.

FIGURE 2.28 *Fitting a fillet in gapped floorboards*

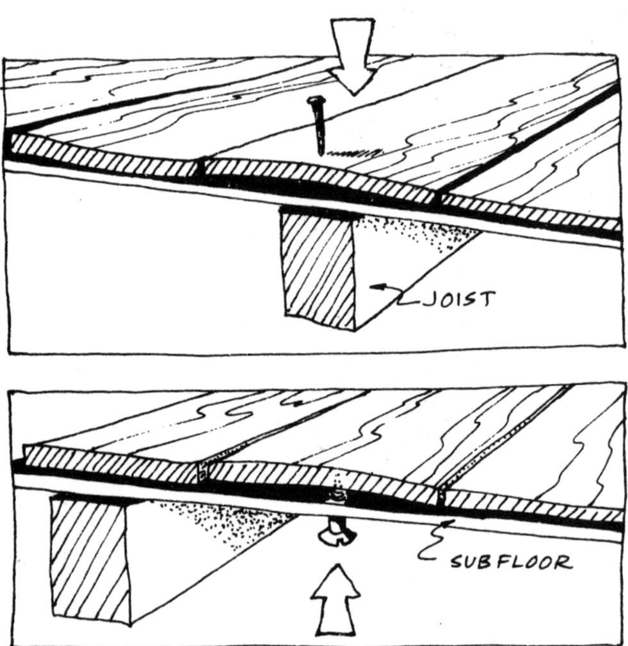

FIGURE 2.29 *Two ways of flattening floorboards*

FIGURE 2.30
Tongue-and-groove flooring

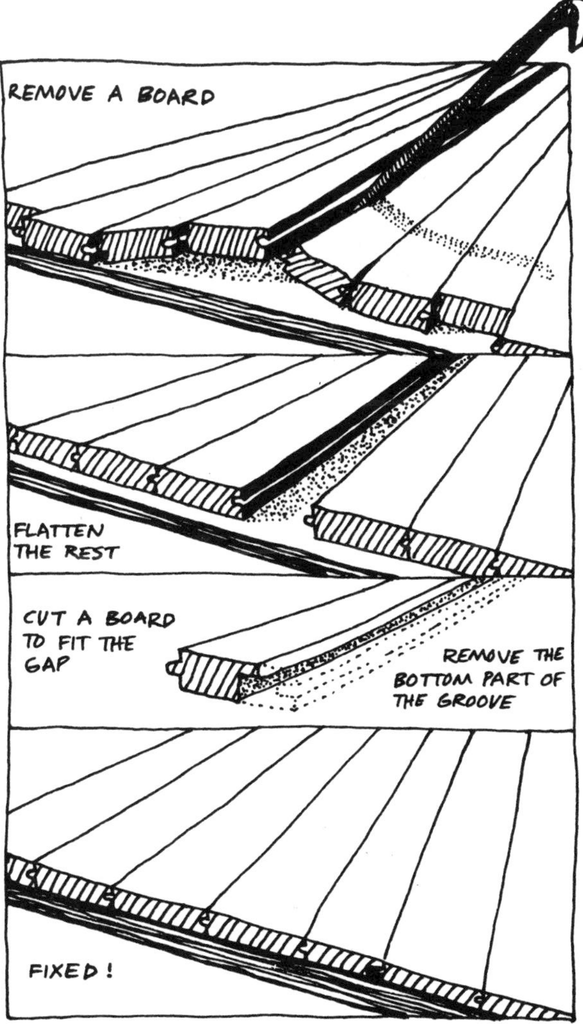

FIGURE 2.31
Replacing a piece of tongue-and-groove flooring

After flattening the remaining boards as described earlier, replace the missing board with a piece fractionally larger than the vacant space—in order to produce a snug fit.

Note that it is necessary to remove the bottom part of the groove (see figure 2.31). This is easily split off with a hammer and a chisel, and doesn't require machinery such as a table saw, although you can use one.

Squeaking. Squeaking floors are usually the result of loose floorboards. If the boards have been surface-nailed, make sure all the nails are hammered home at least flush with the surface of the floor. It would be better to set them a little below the surface using a nail set to avoid making hammer marks—called *moons*—on the floor.

Even if the floor is not surface-nailed, you can try surface-nailing at the squeaking point anyway. Drive two nails at opposing angles and make sure they reach well into the joist below. Set the nails, and fit the holes with plastic wood to match the floor.

Another cure is to wedge the floor from underneath—if you can get to it. Drive the wedges between the squeaking board and the joist on which it is supposed to rest.

Sagging. Sagging can be cured more easily if it occurs on the first

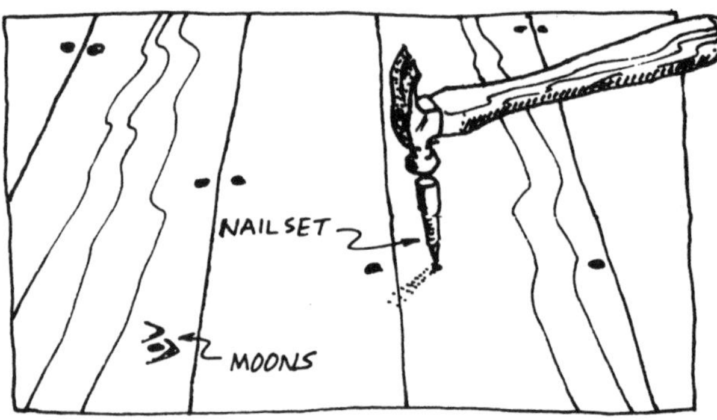

FIGURE 2.32 ***Surface-nailing***

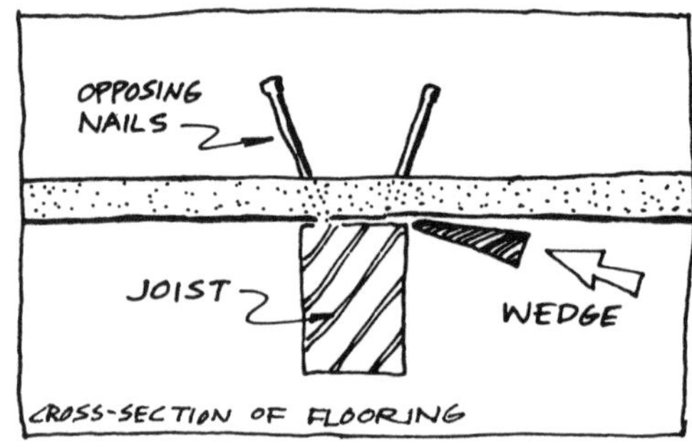

FIGURE 2.33 ***Opposing nails***

floor, for then it may be jacked up level again and permanently supported. If there is sufficient space (as in a basement, but not in a crawl space), you can use the type of metal column that can be adjusted up or down by screwing. The important thing here is to screw it up slowly—no more than ½ inch per week, perhaps at the rate of ¹⁄₁₆ inch a day. This allows everything to readjust gradually without exerting any sudden and potentially damaging strain on the rest of the structure.

If an upper floor is sagging and it's not possible to erect a post under it, there is little you can do short of installing new or additional joists. You can try to rearrange the furniture in the room above so there is as little weight as possible over the sagging area.

STAIRS. Stairs in need of repair can be dangerous as well as annoying, so if there is a stairway in your house, be sure to go over it carefully.

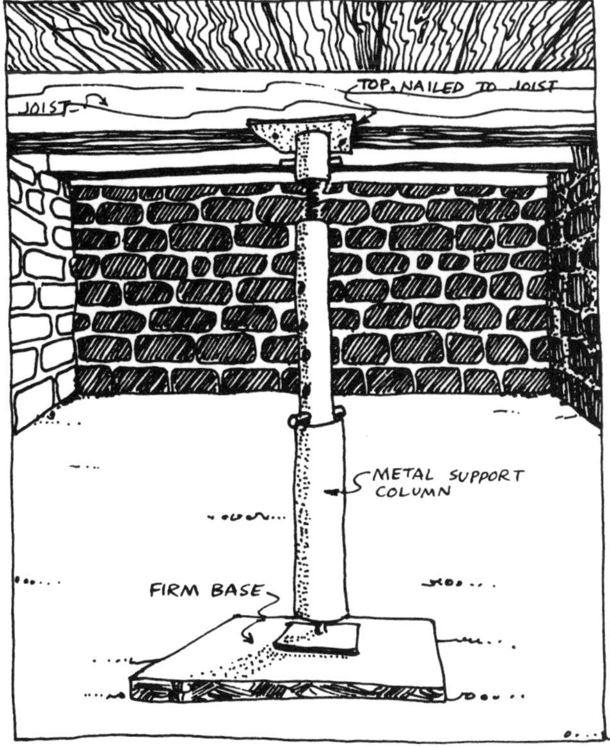

FIGURE 2.34 *Raising a sagging floor*

Assuming the supporting structure is sound (joists or wall framing are not weakened by rot, decay, or excessive loading), the worst problems you are likely to encounter are squeaky treads or loose elements in the balustrade.

Squeaks can sometimes be eliminated by lubricating the offending joint with powdered graphite or even talcum powder. For a more permanent solution, assuming you have access to the underside of the stair, tighten the wedges that can often be found fixed to the undersides of the treads and the risers. Drive the wedges in farther. If there are no wedges, try using short blocks of two-by-two wood screwed to the two adjacent parts that are causing the squeak—usually where the tread meets the riser. If you can't get at the underside of the staircase, you may still be able to stop the squeak by nailing through the surface on either the riser or the tread, whichever part seems to display the most movement—usually the tread.

Handrails, balusters, and other parts of balustrades should all be checked to make sure that there are no broken, missing, or wobbly

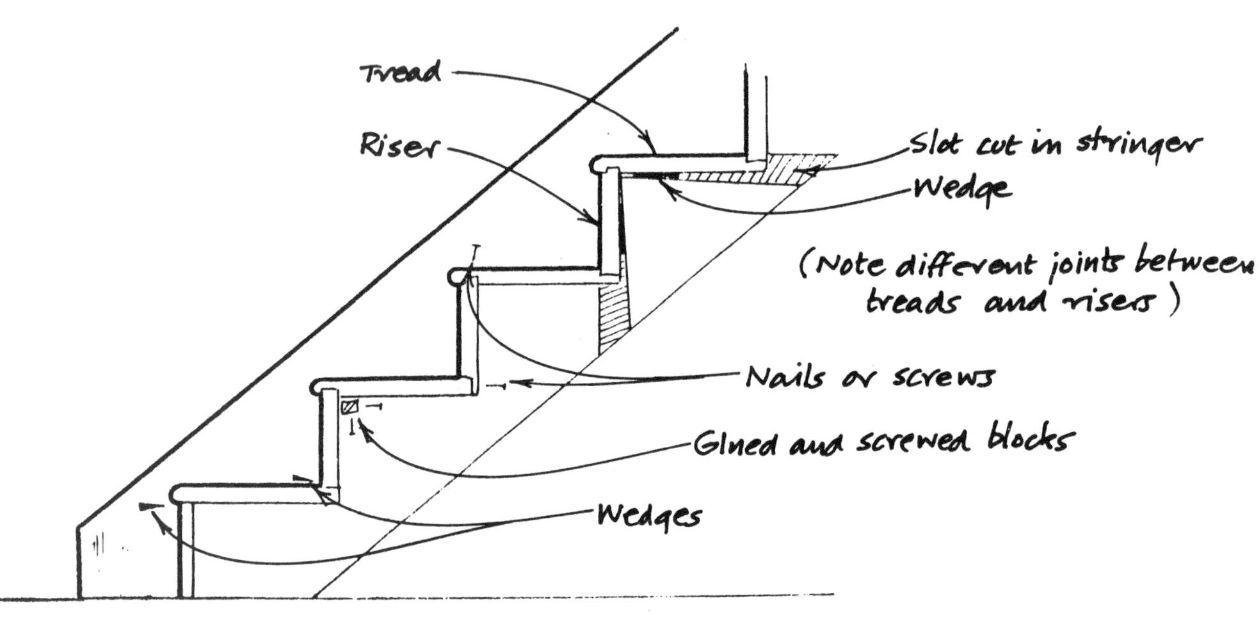

FIGURE 2.35 *Squeak prevention*

parts. They need to be firmly attached if they are to provide any measure of safety.

OTHER WOODWORK AND CABINETRY. Excessive dryness in a house (caused by the heating system, as explained in chapter 9) can affect more than just the major structural elements, such as doors and windows. Over time, other items can deteriorate and hence should be checked occasionally.

If settling or structural sagging has caused doors or windows to stick, they must be removed and refitted. This usually involves having a carpenter plane rails and stiles and possibly graft additional material to the now wrongly shaped items. It is rarely profitable to attempt to realign the openings in which these items fit, but it is important, in order to prevent a worsening of the condition, to correct whatever is causing the sagging or shifting.

A period of very damp weather can cause wood—especially where it is unfinished, such as at the insides of drawers and unpainted door edges—to swell and stick. The proper cure for swollen and stuck doors and drawers is to reduce the moisture content of the article (by lowering the humidity) and then sealing it. As a short-term solution, however, you can make the sticking parts move more easily if you rub them with a dry bar of household soap. Such a treatment is good preventive medicine even if wood drawers are not sticking; it helps them slide more freely.

ADHESIVES. When you're checking the house woodwork, include any wood furniture, especially old furniture. If you find that parts are loose, reglue them. Old woodwork may be glued with animal glues that can become brittle with age and do not always stand up well to heat and dry air.

Look for loose corner blocks on the inside corners of tables, chairs, and cabinets, and loose rungs in chairs, as well as veneers on tabletops and other furniture that may have delaminated.

While you're at it, check other areas where adhesive may have been used—kitchen tiles, for example, on the wall and floor, especially the nonceramic kinds, such as asphalt, rubber, vinyl, or vinyl-asbestos tiles. Anything loose should be reglued.

There are two important things to remember when tackling any

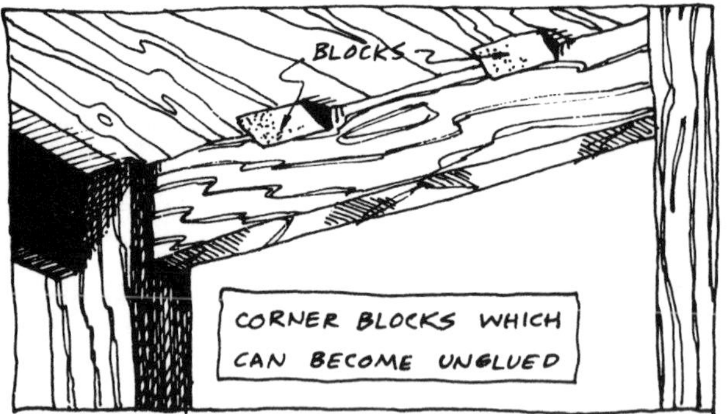

FIGURE 2.36
Corner blocks

gluing job: First, make sure both surfaces are clean—this includes scraping off any traces of old glue. Second, use the right glue for the job.

There are six basic types of glue:

1. *Animal-hide or fish glue.* Now available ready-mixed, this is the old-time glue once exclusively used by cabinetmakers (they had to boil it up in a double gluepot). It works well as long as it is not subject to dampness or excessive heat. However, it can stain light wood and is smelly while being used. It does have one special virtue for use with antiques: it can be removed by means of damp heat so the piece can be worked on again. (More permanent glues can cause damage to a piece if it has to be taken apart.)
2. *White polyvinyl acetate glue.* This is the familiar milky white glue usually sold in squeezable plastic containers. It is good for all interior woodwork where waterproofing is not called for. It is also good for gluing a variety of other materials, such as paper, leather, cork, and fabric.
3. *Plastic resin glue.* This glue comes as a powder that must be mixed with water before use and then forms a strong and waterproof joint for all kinds of woodwork. Joints must be firmly clamped while the glue sets.
4. *Waterproof resorcinol glue.* This two-part glue consists of a powdered catalyst (hardener) and a liquid resin that are mixed

right before use. This glue is ideal for very strong exterior joints.

5. *Epoxy adhesives.* The strongest of all, epoxies are also two-part glues, consisting of resin and catalyst. When set, epoxy is hard, waterproof, and permanent. It is also generally available in small or large quantities, making it ideal for jobs such as gluing china or glass, as well as jobs that involve patching (the epoxy can be used as a filler and then filed down afterward).
6. *Contact cement.* There are two types—a solvent-thinned cement that is very flammable, and a water-thinned variety that is not and that does not give off toxic odors. Since it grips on contact, this cement is especially useful for gluing awkwardly shaped or positioned objects that are not easily clamped. Both surfaces must be allowed to dry for the correct period before being brought together, and they must be perfectly positioned because no adjustment is possible after contact.

In addition to excessive dryness and heat causing glued surfaces to become unstuck, the opposite condition—dampness—can also have the same effect, so run a "gluing check" after an unusually damp period of lengthy spring rains or a long spell of humid weather.

HARDWARE. An important contribution to the proper functioning of the interior fittings of a house is made by the hardware used to hold things together and to allow them to open and close where needed. Take a moment to check that all attached hardware is in good operating order.

Exterior locks, for example, can freeze and become inoperable in the extreme cold. It is tiresome to stand in the cold, trying to warm up a key over a match (usually with a wind blowing) in order to melt a frozen door lock (by inserting the hot key into it). So practice a little periodic prevention: apply liquid graphite to the key and work it in and out of all your exterior locks. Graphite has a twofold effect: it helps prevent freezing and provides general lubrication, which will make the lock last longer and be easier to operate.

A lock that is still hard to operate after lubrication may need

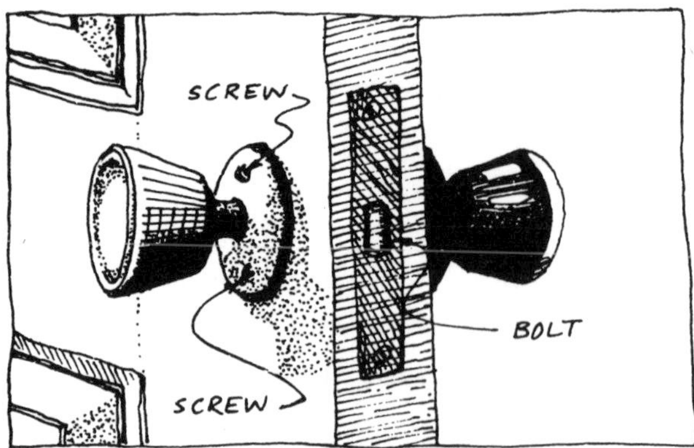

FIGURE 2.37 *Tubular lock*

cleaning. Carefully remove and disassemble the lock, and clean it thoroughly with an old toothbrush and some solvent such as paint thinner, mineral spirits, methylated spirits, turpentine, or even lacquer thinner—but be sure to heed the various cautions on the label, especially with the more toxic substances such as lacquer thinner. On reassembly, lightly lubricate the lock and try again. If it's still hard to work, it's either improperly assembled (you may have screwed something in too tightly) or too old and worn, and should be replaced.

Pay particular attention to tubular locks (see figure 2.37); the retaining screws sometimes work loose. If you have to tighten them, make sure that the bolt still springs in and out easily—that it does not bind because you have tightened the screws too much.

On your lock inspection tour, carry a screwdriver and make sure the screws holding the hinges for doors, windows, and cabinets are tight. It is surprising how easily some of these screws can work loose: that can lead to hard-to-close or hard-to-open doors and windows. Some hinges have removable pins, which hold the two leaves together. These sometimes work up and threaten to fall out. Tap them back in.

Use the screwdriver to check that all the catches, locks, handles, and fasteners around each room are still tightly screwed in place. Many of the wood handles on drawers and doors are held by screws that may need to be tightened. If glued in place, they should be checked and reglued if necessary.

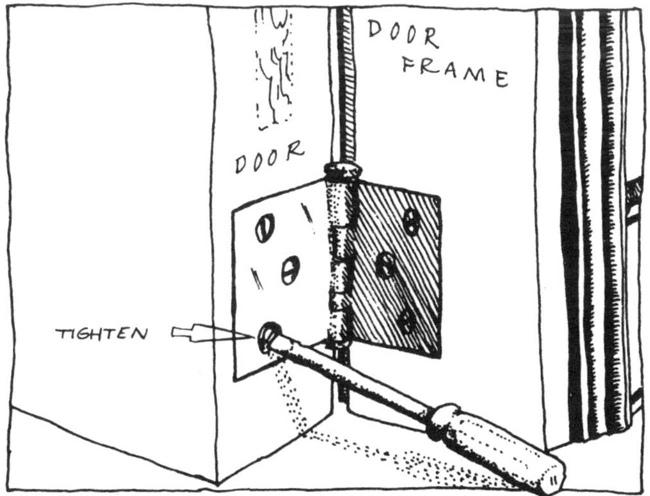

FIGURE 2.38 *Tightening hinge screws*

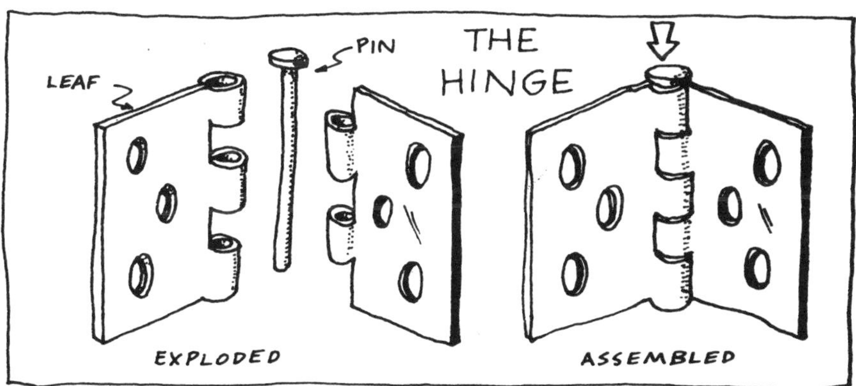

FIGURE 2.39 *Hinge parts*

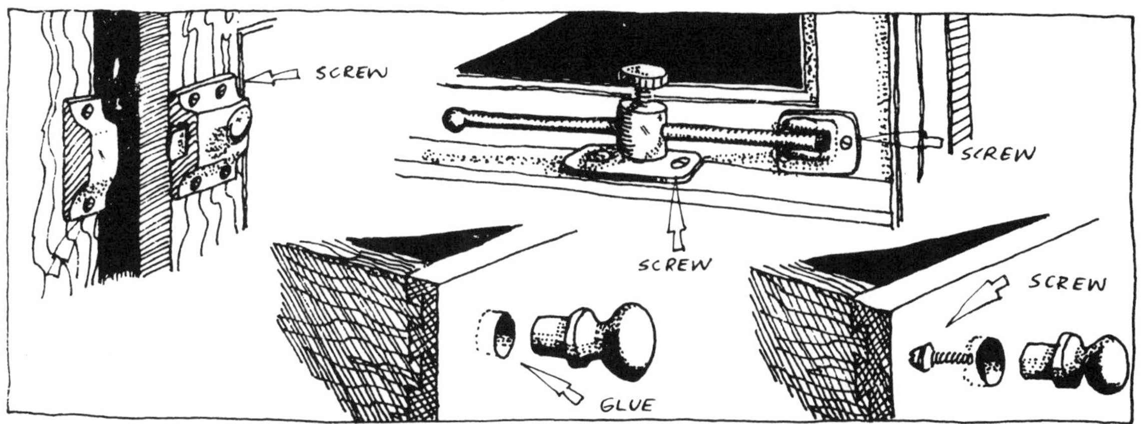

FIGURE 2.40 *Hardware checks*

THREE

Systems Inspections

Having checked the basic structural components of the house, you should now focus on the two main systems that provide the basic utilities of a building—the electricity and the plumbing.

THE ELECTRICAL SYSTEM

Practically all of us are now dependent on electricity. When the power goes out, much of what makes a house run comes to a standstill. Although it's not necessary to be an expert in how an electrical system works, you should be familiar with the important components and know where they are in your house—and how to react safely during an emergency.

Fuses and Circuit Breakers

There is one golden rule for working with electricity: *Never* do anything until you're sure the power is off. That means learning about the fuse box and where it's located—for it is here that fuses or circuit breakers and the main supply control are found.

In older houses, the fuse box is typically located in some dark corner, such as a cupboard under the stairs; in more recent houses, the fuse box is usually accessible in the basement. Never stand on a wet or damp floor when working with the fuse box. This advice is particularly applicable if the fuse box is in a basement where dampness and standing water are not unknown. Stand on some dry boards instead.

Ideally, everything should be clearly marked and labeled in the fuse box. You should be able to open the door and see at a glance the main breaker switch or lever (which turns off the power to the box

FIGURE 3.1 *Fuse box location*

itself) and a row of switches or fuses designated as controlling the power to different parts of the house—such as kitchen range, bedroom, furnace, hot-water heater, living room. The purpose of this setup is to enable you to correct a problem with one circuit without turning off the power to the whole house.

If switches or fuses are not clearly marked—and if there is no separate list or diagram—mark them carefully yourself while everything is in good working order. You might call in an electrician to trace the circuits, but actually you can do it yourself by deductive trial-and-error experimentation. Turn everything on in the house and then note what goes off as you turn off each fuse or switch in sequence. Have some simple lamp or appliance available so you can check the power at each plug-in outlet.

Cutting off the power to each circuit can be done by either a fuse or a circuit breaker. Both will interrupt the flow of electricity—either

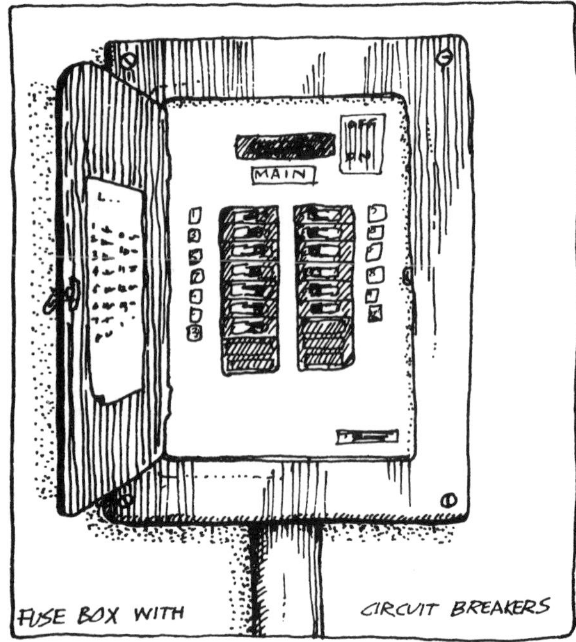

FIGURE 3.2 *Fuse box*

because something has gone wrong on that circuit or because you want to work on that circuit.

Fuses today are most commonly one of three types (see figure 3.3). The *plug fuse* has a visible metal strip inside a glass screw-in unit. The metal strip melts and breaks when the circuit is overloaded, and the glass usually becomes blackened. The fuse should be replaced by one of the same amperage (noted on the fuse). The *dual element fuse* has a spring-loaded metal strip that permits temporary overloading, such as when an electric motor starts up, but otherwise it operates like a plug fuse. The *cartridge fuse* has no visible evidence that it has "blown." The only way to know is to replace it with a fuse you know is good.

With circuit breakers the situation is greatly simplified. These switches trip into the off position when the circuit they control is overloaded. There are two types: one trips all the way into the off position and needs simply to be switched on again; the other trips only halfway—you must switch it off completely before you can return it to the on position. (You don't need to switch off the main power to reset either type of circuit breaker.)

FIGURE 3.3 *Fuse types*

FIGURE 3.4 *Circuit breakers*

If you like the idea of circuit breakers but your house is equipped with plug fuses, you can replace them with so-called button breakers. These look just like screw-in plug fuses, but they have a button sticking out of the center. When this kind of breaker trips, the button pops out; all you need do is to push it back in to reset the circuit.

When something electrical stops working, the first job is to identify which fuse has blown. If you've previously made a careful list of the circuits, that should be easy. If you haven't, you'll have to examine each fuse. (If you have circuit breakers, you can see immediately which one has gone off.) Having first turned off the items you know are on that circuit, shut off the main power, making sure you are not standing on a wet floor and that you have a flashlight handy. Then unscrew or remove the fuse in question and replace it with a new fuse of the same amperage. Now turn everything back on. It is a good idea to have on hand extra fuses of the type in your box; checking this stock should be a routine chore.

The commonest reason for a blown fuse is overloading, too much going on at the same time. If, after replacing the fuse, it blows again with fewer items drawing power, there may be damage somewhere. Check each appliance on the circuit for visibly defective wiring or plugs, and plug each appliance in turn into another low-use circuit to see whether it is the appliance that is causing the blown fuse. If this test does not provide any answers, it is time to call in a qualified professional.

Grounding

You don't have to be an electrician to understand grounding. It means simply that if an electrical malfunction occurs in the house, any loose electricity will be carried by the ground wire back to the fuse box and from there to a rod set in the ground. This precaution keeps you from being the conductor of that electricity to the ground, thus saving you from potentially damaging results. Grounding of electrical outlets is something you can and should check.

Modern outlets have three holes—the third one is for the ground. This is matched by the three-pronged plug on modern appliances. Such a plug in such an outlet (assuming it is wired correctly inside) provides you with protection in case the appliance malfunctions.

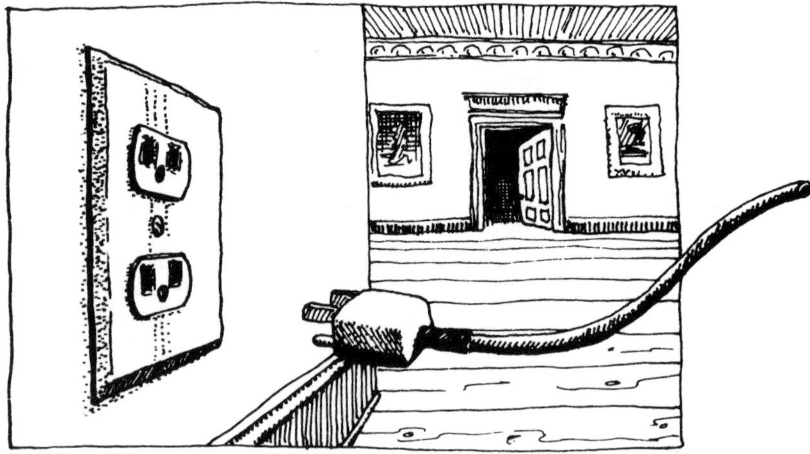

FIGURE 3.5 *Three-hole outlet and plug*

Older outlets, which have only two holes, may also be grounded inside, but you must use an adapter before you can plug in a three-pronged plug. The adapter allows you to put a three-pronged plug into a two-hole outlet, but it does not provide any grounding protection unless you connect the pigtail to the center screw of the outlet cover.

FIGURE 3.6 ***Grounding adapter***

An appliance with a two-pronged plug may not be grounded, but if your outlets are grounded you can still achieve protection by using a Ground Fault Interrupter (GFI). You can have an electrician replace existing outlets in places where you are likely to use nongrounded appliances (such as in the kitchen or the bathroom) with GFIs, or you can use portable GFIs that simply plug into any three-hole outlet.

All of the foregoing assumes that the outlets are grounded. If they are not, you are unprotected no matter how many prongs your plugs have. You can check your outlets easily. All you need is a test light, available at any hardware store. Simply insert one lead of the test

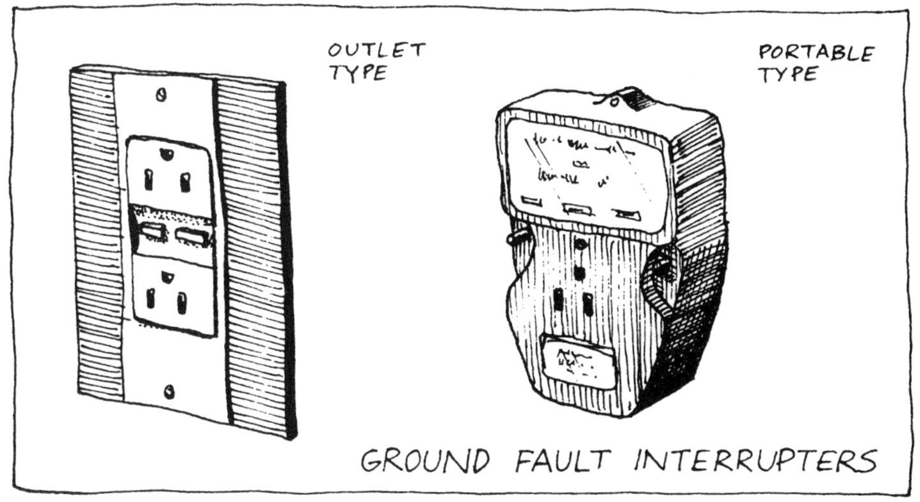

FIGURE 3.7 ***Ground fault interrupters***

light into the hot-wire slot and the other lead either into the third hole or, if there are only two holes, onto the face-plate screw (see figure 3.8). (Either might be the hot-wire slot; try the left one first, then the right one.) The light should glow. If it does not, you don't have a grounded outlet, and you should have it rewired or replaced with a known grounded outlet. Perform the grounding test on every outlet in the house.

Before doing any work on a wired-in outlet or fixture, cut off the power to that circuit. Make a further check with the test light to be sure that the power is off at an outlet before exposing its inner workings.

Repairs

Most electrical repairs are best left to a qualified electrician, but there are two common repairs that can be undertaken by anyone who exercises a little care. One is replacing wires and a plug on an

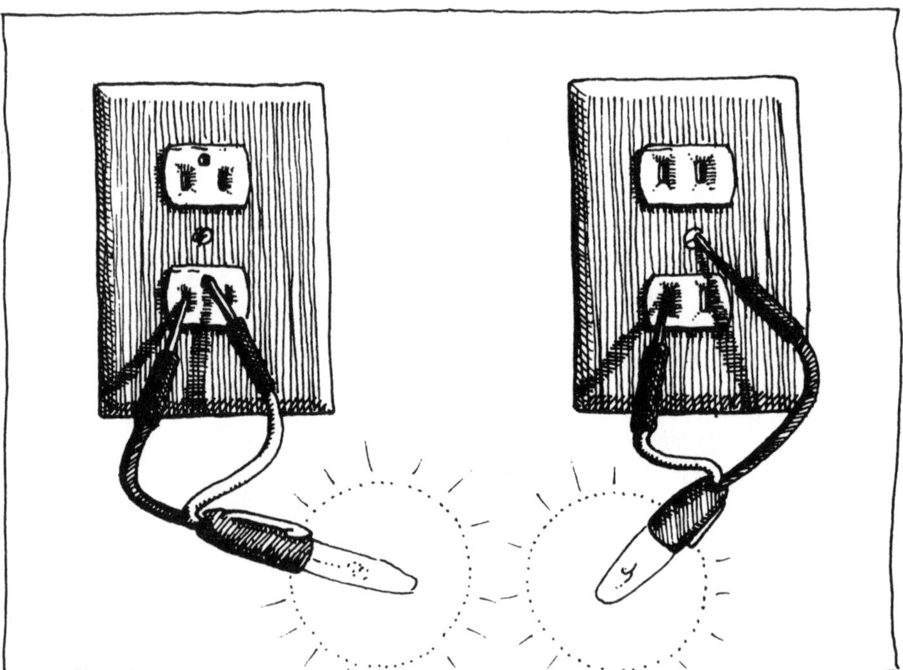

FIGURE 3.8 *Proof of grounding*

appliance or extension cord; the other is rewiring a lamp. First, make a regular electrical check of these items. Frayed wires, chipped or cracked plugs, bare wire showing anywhere—all of these conditions mean the appliances should not be used until they are repaired.

There are four common types of repairable plugs for lamps and small electric appliances. By replacing any of these with plugs of the same type, you will avoid danger from using an inappropriate plug.

1. *The lever-release type.* Pull up the lever in the base of the plug, insert the wire as far as it will go (be sure its flat shape conforms to the oval opening), and press the lever back into place. The two sharp teeth will bite into the two sides of the wire and make contact.
2. *The case type.* Separate the case from the prongs by pressing the prongs together and pulling on them. Cut the wire squarely across the end, and insert through the base of the case. Pull the prongs apart, and insert the wire into the base of the prongs as far as it will go. Squeeze the prongs back together—again, this action forces the teeth through the wire—and push the prongs back in the case until there is a slight catch.
3. *The two-pronged screw-terminal type.* Remove the insulating cap (see figure 3.10), insert the wire through the base of the plug, and make an underwriters' knot. (Follow the illustration carefully. This knot is designed to relieve any strain on the wire connections.) Now connect the wires securely to the screw terminals, and replace the insulating cap. It does not matter which wire is connected to which terminal.
4. *The three-pronged grounded plug.* Start by attaching the green (or bare) wire to the green or largest terminal. This is the grounding wire. Once this is done, the procedure is the same as for a two-pronged plug.

Typical lamp socket rewiring is shown in figure 3.12. Not all lamps are wired in exactly the same way. There are numerous ingenious variations, starting with the way the socket comes apart—it may be snapped open, which is usually indicated by the words *press here* stamped on the case, or it may need to be unscrewed, which the

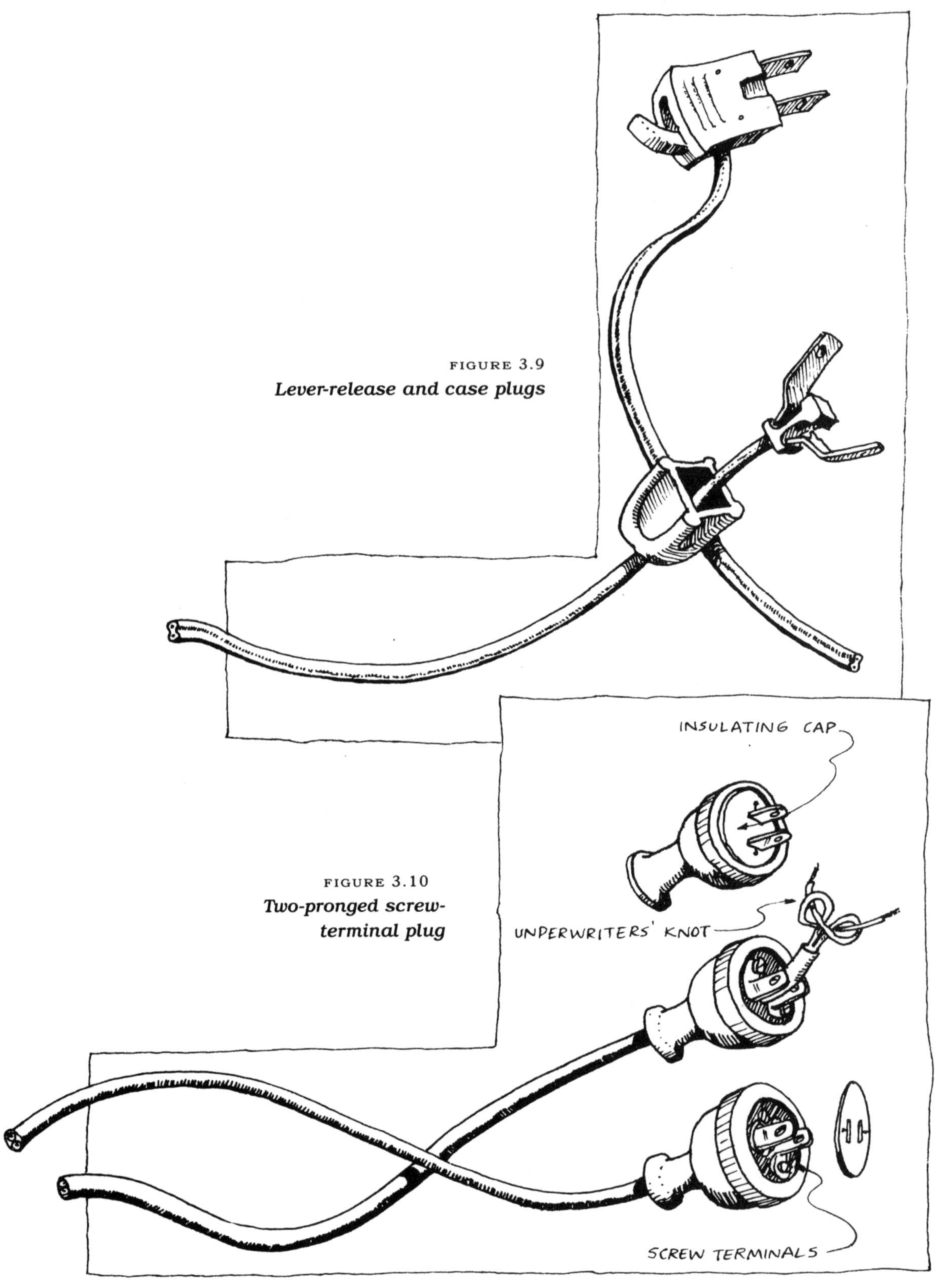

FIGURE 3.9
Lever-release and case plugs

FIGURE 3.10
Two-pronged screw-terminal plug

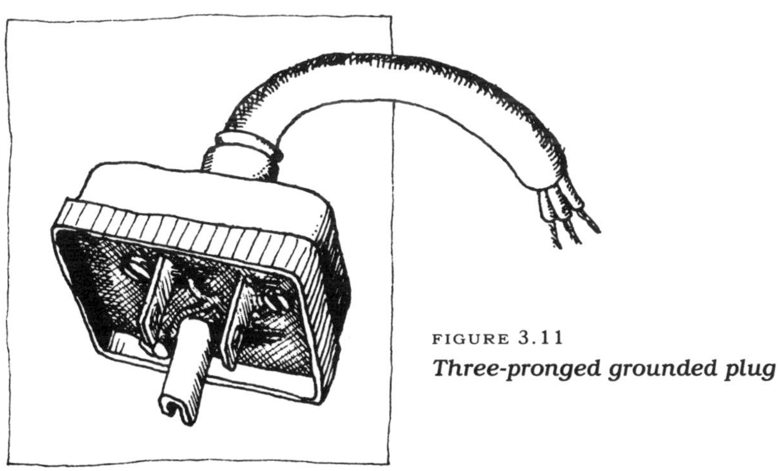

FIGURE 3.11
Three-pronged grounded plug

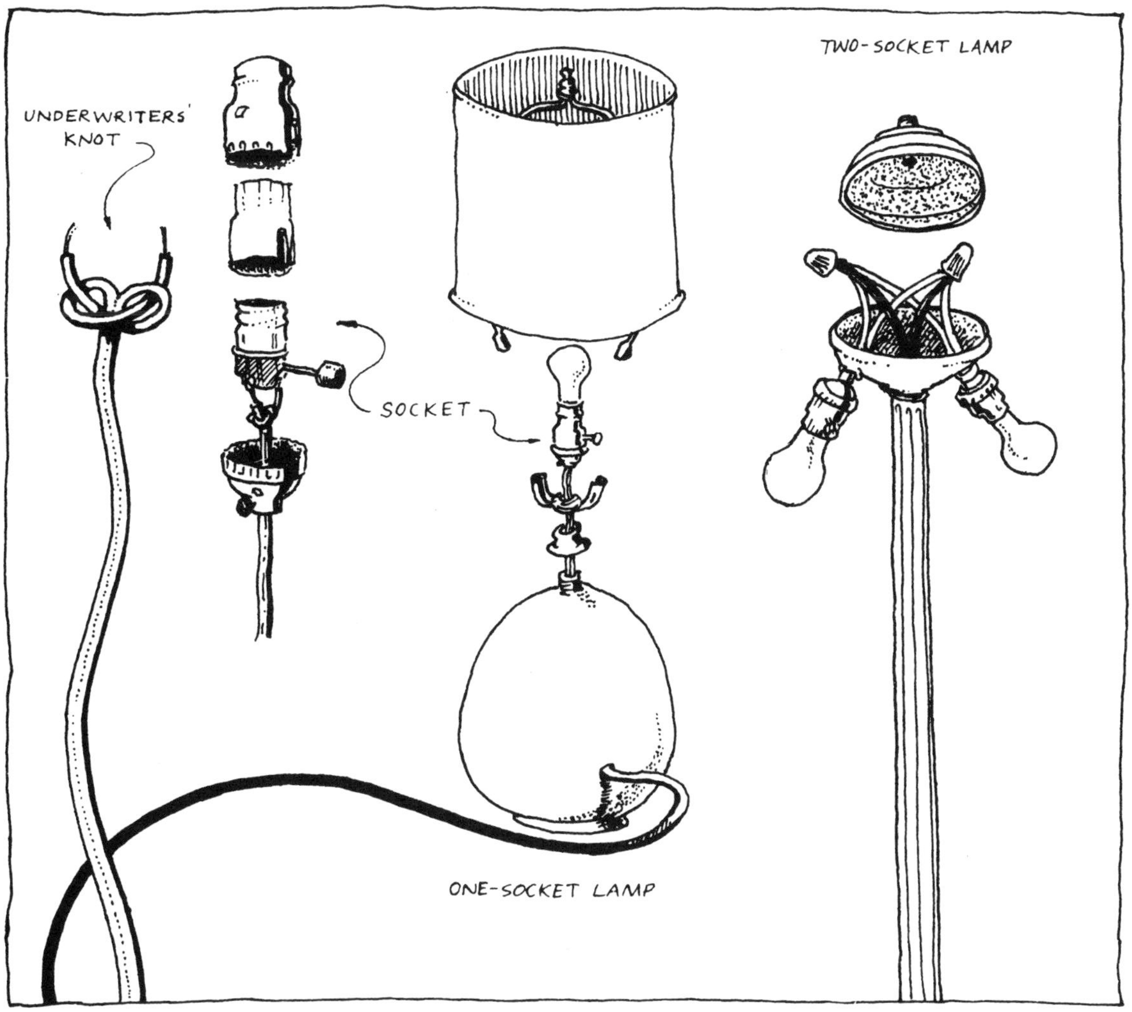

UNDERWRITERS' KNOT
SOCKET
ONE-SOCKET LAMP
TWO-SOCKET LAMP

FIGURE 3.12 *Lamp rewiring*

presence of a small screw should make obvious. Other differences may include the way the harp—the piece to which a shade may be attached—can be taken off. The differences are too numerous to catalog, but anyone curious enough to investigate will usually be able to fathom this mystery.

One final caution: avoid the excessive use of plug-in cubes and extension cords to add more items to the standard two-plug outlet. It is easy to overload a circuit, causing a short and, possibly, a fire. Make the inspection of outlets a part of your annual check.

THE PLUMBING SYSTEM

The plumbing system of a house comprises more components than you might think. It includes not only the pipes that bring water to the various fixtures around the house and the pipes that carry it away, but also the well, pressure tank, and other parts involved in the supply, as well as heaters, purifiers, the waste system, and, of course, all the fixtures themselves.

The Water Supply

Most homes in the United States use water supplied by a municipal septum. The only important thing for a homeowner to know is the location of the main shutoff valve—the one you should turn off if you have any major leaks or burst pipes. *Make sure you know where it is even if you have to call in a plumber to help locate it.*

Knowing exactly how to turn off the water and the electricity is vital in an emergency. You may never want to do any repairs yourself, but if you can shut down these systems, you can prevent a simple problem from turning into a catastrophe.

Rural homes and some suburban homes have their own water supply systems. Such a system should be checked at least once a year. Don't take it for granted—you run the risk of it failing at an inopportune moment.

In an individual supply system, the water will usually be pumped up from a well or drawn from a spring or stream. There will generally be a pressure tank between the source and the house, unless the house is gravity fed. In a gravity-fed house, the source is sufficiently higher than the house for the water's own weight to build up enough pressure to run the system.

Even in a house with its own water supply, you must know how to shut it off. If you have a pressure tank, you have a choice: you can shut off the water going into the tank or coming out of it. If you need to drain the system in the entire house (because, for example, you're closing it up for the winter), turn off the supply *before* it goes into the pressure tank and drain everything, including the tank itself. If it's just a question of working on one section of the plumbing in the house, you can turn off the valve controlling the flow coming *out* of the pressure tank.

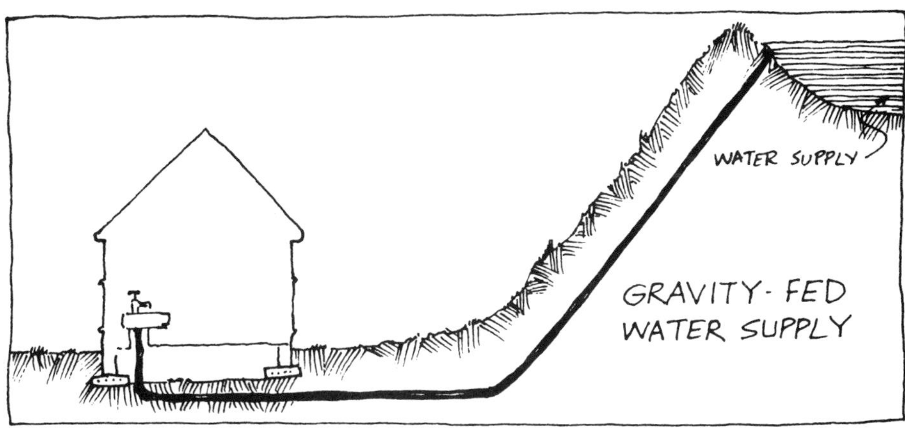

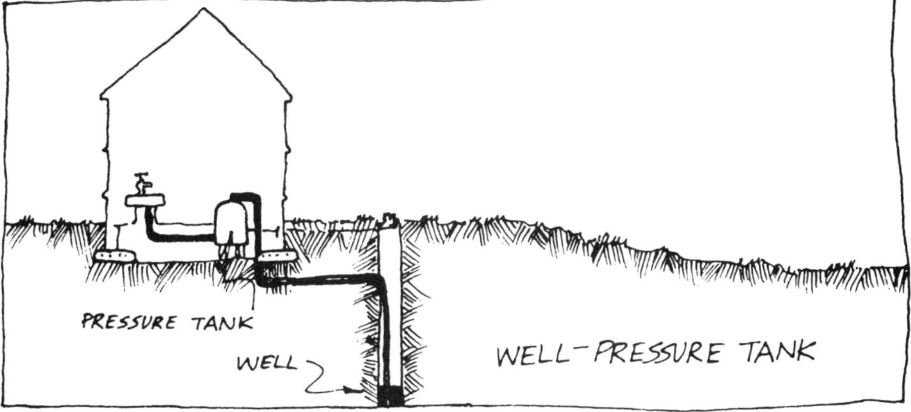

FIGURE 3.13 *Water supplies*

a This valve controls the flow into the tank. The pipe goes from the tank to the well, probably disappearing through the wall or into the floor.

b This valve controls the flow out of the tank. The pipe runs from the tank to the hot-water heater and other pipes around the house.

c The pressure gauge.

d The reset button.

e The electricity switch.

FIGURE 3.14 *Pressure tank controls*

It is also possible, of course, that you may be able to turn off the water closer to the involved section, since many plumbing fixtures have their own shut-off valves—look under the bathroom sink, for example. Many houses have valves in the system that control the supply to zones in the house and that can be shut off so you don't have to shut off the main valve.

Once you know how to turn off the water supply, the next thing to know is how to turn it on again. This is simple enough if you are supplied by a municipal water system, but if a pressure tank is involved, you may have to do more than just turn the appropriate

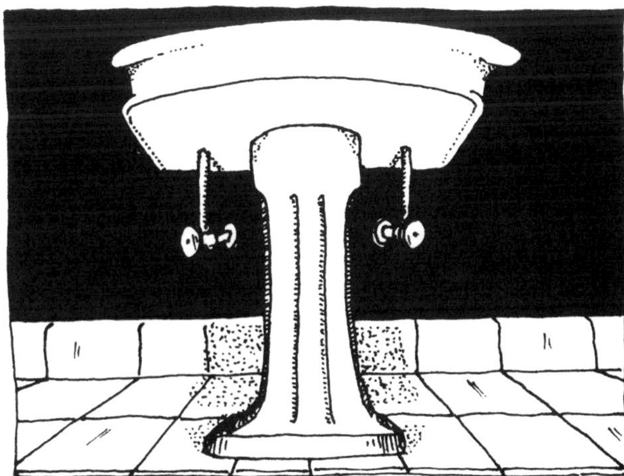

FIGURE 3.15 *Typical bathroom sink shut-off valves*

valve. The function of the pressure tank is twofold: to activate the well pump when required, and to supply water to the house at sufficient pressure. Various problems can arise if there's too much or too little pressure. Become familiar with the normal readings on the gauge, which is usually located somewhere on the tank. It registers the pressure inside the tank in pounds per square inch (PSI).

A drop in pressure in the tank (because you have drawn off water somewhere in the system) activates a switch that starts the well pump, sending more water into the tank. When there is once again sufficient water in the tank, the pressure will have risen enough to shut off the pump.

If the pump keeps running and the pressure does not rise, you may have an empty well or a leak. Turn off the switch supplying electricity to the pump, and call the plumber. If the pump were to run continuously, it would eventually burn out.

Starting up the pump is easier. Once you've made sure the electricity is on and the valve is open, simply hold down the reset button for 15 or 20 seconds. The pump should start, and continue to run after you release the button. The pressure should rise to about 40 PSI and stay there after the pump stops. You then have a full tank.

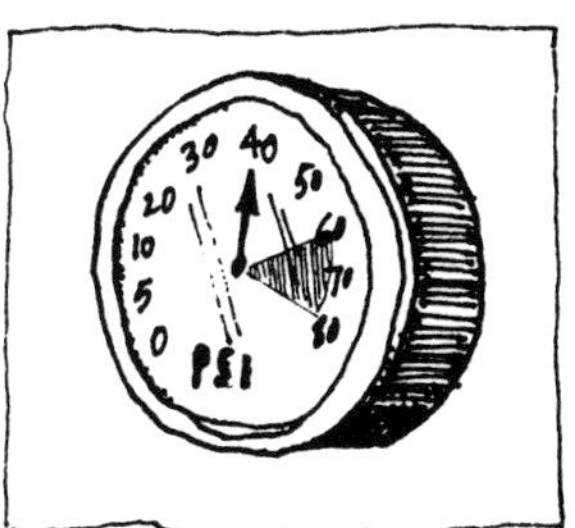

FIGURE 3.16
Pressure gauge

During your periodic check, inspect for leaks and make sure that the pump does not run continuously and that the pressure gauge reads about 40 PSI. In areas of freezing weather, check that the whole system, from well to pressure tank, is sufficiently insulated.

Well Checks

To check the condition and efficiency of the well, run the water in the house for 20 minutes or so. The pump should go on and off, the pressure should hold steady, and the water should stay clear. If it maintains this performance in the driest part of the year, you have a good well. But if the water slows to a trickle or turns brown, you may not have enough water for your needs. Once a year, have the quality of the water checked at your local health office. Before taking the sample from a household faucet, hold a match under the faucet (to kill any bacteria). Now let the faucet run for a few minutes before taking your sample.

Hot-Water Heater

An important component of a home's water system is the hot-water heater. Unless you have hot water supplied from the central heating system or some kind of solar installation, the water is probably heated in a separate tank. These tanks are generally fueled by electricity or gas, though there are also oil-fired heaters. Usually these appliances are among the most trouble-free in the house and require little maintenance.

Recently installed hot-water heaters should be partly drained once a year (after turning off the fuel source) to flush out accumulated sediment. The drain valve is typically located near the bottom of the tank and usually is threaded so you can attach a hose to it and run off the water into a convenient drain. Simply open the drain valve and let the water run until it turns clear. However, if you have an old tank or have not performed this operation for a long time, try the valve carefully before opening it. If it's frozen into position, opening it may make resealing it impossible. You could then have a leak requiring professional repair.

Check the hot-water heater also for the correct thermostat setting. The lower the temperature of the water maintained in the heater, the cheaper it is to run the heater. If the water is so hot that you mix in

FIGURE 3.17 *Water heaters*

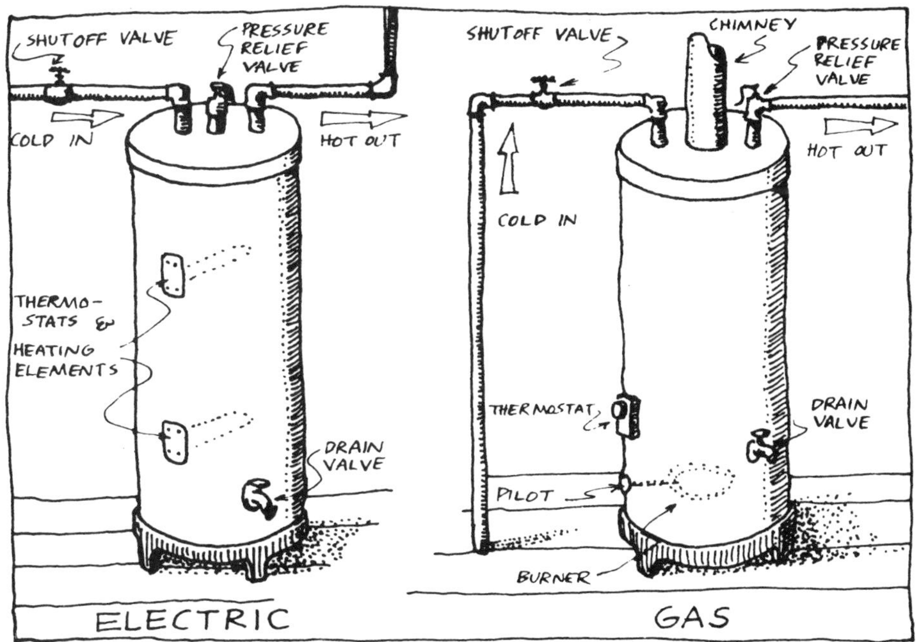

cold water each time you draw hot, you are wasting money and energy. Gas hot-water heaters have only one thermostat to adjust, but most electric hot-water heaters have two, an upper and a lower. If you adjust only one, the other will simply take up the slack.

Gas hot-water heaters should have the pilot light orifice and burner area cleaned out periodically. Also check that the chimney venting the burner is in good condition and sufficiently insulated where it passes through any walls, ceilings, or roofs. Inspect the point at which the vent passes through the building; the immediate area should not be hot to the touch. Naturally, there should be no gas leaks; check by smell, not by waving a lighted match around (most gas has an odor added to aid in leak detection).

The last thing to check is the pressure relief valve. Many heaters have one, usually at the top (see figure 3.17). Its name explains its purpose. It is designed to leak should pressure build up inside the tank—and thus prevent an explosion. If it leaks continuously, call a professional to do the repairs. The valve may be faulty, or there may actually be something wrong inside the tank.

The Septic System

If the plumbing wastes from your house drain into municipal sewers, you don't have to bother with this. If you have your own septic system, the time to check the efficiency of the drain field is during very wet weather. If the system is working correctly, the waste goes into the septic tank, where bacteria break down the solids, leaving liquid to flow out into a drain field. This area—also called a leaching field—consists of perforated pipe laid in beds of gravel beneath the ground.

The size and composition of the leaching field should be sufficient to absorb the waste water without turning the area into a marsh. But if the ground is not porous enough, if the field is too small, or if the pipes have clogged up, heavy rain can well overload the system. The resulting boggy area will tell you that improvements are needed, perhaps additional lengths of drainage pipe.

If the boggy area also smells of sewage, you may have an additional problem. A properly functioning septic tank large enough for the house and its household should need no attention and should not smell. If it becomes overloaded, however, or if too much non-biodegradable detergent kills the necessary bacteria, it will have to be pumped out. Look in the yellow pages under Septic Tank Pumping to get this done professionally, usually with a minimum of fuss and disturbance to you, the system, or the grounds. Beware of the pumper's certain insistence on returning at frequent intervals. This procedure can be avoided if you use only biodegradable detergents and feed the bacteria a spoonful or two of yeast once in a while—just flush it down the toilet.

FIGURE 3.18 *Typical septic system*

FIGURE 3.19 *Drain field extension*

There are ways to bypass the problem altogether, which are more applicable when building a new house. But in the event your system becomes incapacitated, they deserve mention.

First, toilets do not need to be connected to a septic tank (although in some localities old-fashioned building codes still insist on it). There are toilets that perform their own composting operation in self-contained tanks, usually kept in the basement, and that need be emptied only once a year—at which time all you take out is odorless garden compost. Not only ecologically beneficial, these composting toilets greatly reduce the use of the septic tank and dramatically reduce your water consumption, since they do not use any.

Second, many people use two separate septic tanks, one for solid waste and the other for "gray water." Gray water is water from dishwashers, washing machines, showers, and tubs. By keeping these separate, the gray water, which does not contain solid wastes needing to be broken down, may be leached off without overloading the main septic tank.

A third method constitutes a compromise between the old and the new. It involves replacing the traditional flush toilet with a newer design needing much less water to be operated. In fact, in some dry areas of the United States where water conservation is increasingly important, it is now mandatory that all new toilets be of this variety.

Plumbing Fixtures

To complete the check of the plumbing system, all that remains now is to inspect the plumbing fixtures themselves. Make sure that all the faucets shut off with no continuing drips, that there are no leaks in the drains, traps, or waste lines, and that everything does in fact drain away efficiently. If you should discover any of the following problems, they can usually be repaired quite easily.

DRIPPING FAUCETS. Most faucets can be divided into two types: faucets with washers and washerless faucets. The more modern washerless faucets often seem to have been designed to make disassembly by the uninitiated as difficult as possible, since the various nuts and screws that hold the things together are usually very hard to find—hidden under snapcaps, for example.

Nevertheless, drips usually originate from one of only three locations. If water drips out of the spout no matter how hard you turn the tap, the washer or its seat is worn. If water leaks out of the base of the handle, the packing nut is either loose or its washer or packing material is worn. If water appears at the base of the faucet, then the coupling nut, which connects the plumbing to the faucet under the sink, is defective.

Without a basin wrench it can be very hard to rectify the last type of leak. Moreover, since an effective repair may involve disconnecting the pipe in order to replace the washers, this job is probably best left to a professional. The first two leaks, however, can be tackled with little more than a screwdriver and a common adjustable wrench:

Turn off the water supply. Remove the tap or handle (the screw that holds this on may be visible or hidden under a decorative cap). Next, possibly also hidden under a decorative housing, is the packing nut. If this is the source of your leak, tightening it may cure the problem. Alternatively, it may need a new washer.

Once the packing nut is removed, you can screw the handle back on, and by turning it as if you were turning the water on, the valve stem will come out. At the bottom of the valve stem is the washer, which is screwed in place by a small brass screw. When replacing the washer, be sure to use a new washer of exactly the right size.

TOILET TANK PROBLEMS. The most common problem encountered with toilet tanks is that they refuse to stop running. This may be due to a malfunctioning inlet valve, a faulty float ball, or its more modern counterpart, the plastic float.

The inlet valve, which is opened when the tank is flushed and closed by either the plastic float or the float ball when the tank is full again, relies on rubber, fiber, or plastic washers to effect a complete seal. If you can hold the plastic float or the float ball up and water still comes through the inlet valve, it either needs new washers or, more easily done but more expensive, needs to be replaced.

If the plastic float or the float ball does not rise high enough, it will not shut off the inlet valve. The newer plastic float must then be replaced, but the older float ball can sometimes be bent down on its rod so that it shuts off the inlet valve at a lower level. If either leaks, it should be replaced.

When the toilet is flushed, a trip lever removes a device that controls entry of water into the bowl. This device may be either a rubber ball on the end of a rod or chain, or a plastic flapper. As the water flows into the tank again, these devices should settle back over the inlet and completely seal it. If they are misaligned or worn and leaky, water will continually flow into the bowl. This will be evidenced by continuous ripples on the surface of the water in the bowl and a possible "singing" of the inlet valve as it attempts in vain to fill up the tank. Misalignment can usually be corrected by the proper bending of the various guide rods, but wear is remedied only by replacement.

The opposite problem—not enough water—is usually the result of a partially blocked inlet valve. Try jiggling it to remove any sediment. If this fails, replace it—but first check that the plastic float or float ball is dropping when the tank is flushed (and so opening the inlet valve properly).

BLOCKED SINK. The U-shaped pipe found below most sinks is designed to hold water, which prevents sewer gases from entering the house. It can easily become filled with more solid matter, resulting in a blocked sink.

To clean the trap, begin by unscrewing the cleanout plug located under the lowest part of the trap. Remember to have a bucket handy, and if the blockage does not immediately gush out, poke a wire coat hanger, with a little hook bent in the end, up both sides of the trap. If this does not produce results, undo the slip nuts holding the U-section to the sink and the rest of the plumbing and remove it completely to make sure it is perfectly clean. This is the place where most blockages occur. Should the sink still refuse to drain after you have

FIGURE 3.20 *Vent stack*

replaced the trap and refilled the sink, try using a plunger before calling a plumber.

Other Parts of the Plumbing System

The check of the plumbing system should include not only the obvious sinks, tubs, shower stalls, and toilet fixtures, but also the dishwasher, washing machine, sprinkler system, and all outside faucets.

One often forgotten part of the plumbing system is the vent stack (or stacks). This is a pipe that rises from the main drain of the house and usually exits high on the roof. It provides an escape for air and sewer gas that might otherwise find their way into the house. It also prevents air locks from blocking the draining of various fixtures. It is worth inspecting the top of the pipe once in a while to make sure that it has not become clogged in any way by birds' nests or other debris.

FOUR

Cosmetic Maintenance

Late spring is the ideal time to inspect, touch up, or even redo the surface finishes of a house.

THE EXTERIOR

When winter is finally gone, and before summer arrives, take a look at the paint on the outside of the house. How it is wearing can tell you a lot about the condition of your house. It can also tell you whether you simply need to repaint or whether you've got to make some structural changes first. Exterior paint is designed to shed water from the outside, but if moisture is allowed to seep into the wall and dampen the wood behind the paint, then blisters, bubbles, and peeling will occur, no matter how many times you repaint. The moisture problem must be solved first. Check for all the possible causes: defective caulking or leaky gutters (see chapter 1), corroded flashing (see chapter 2), or poor vapor barriers inside the house (see chapter 9).

Sometimes all seems to be in order, and yet the paint still peels. In this case, small louvers inserted in the siding are often sufficient to ventilate the area behind it. A 1-inch louver inserted in each closed-off area between framing members, especially over windows, is usually enough. The framing members in most houses are 16 inches apart and can be located by the vertical rows of nails in the siding.

If only the top layer of paint has peeled—revealing old paint beneath—then the most recent coat of paint was applied to a dirty or damp surface. Never paint unless the following conditions obtain:

1. The temperature is between 50° and 90°.
2. The surface is dry and clean.
3. Old peeling areas have been scraped away.
4. Cracks and holes (including nailhead holes) have been caulked or filled.
5. Damaged or rotted wood has been replaced.
6. The paint to be used is applicable over the existing paint.

This last is especially important because, without proper preparation, certain types of paints cannot be successfully applied over other

FIGURE 4.1 *Siding ventilation*

types. For example, latex paints will not do well over oil paints, and oil paints will not do well over so-called self-chalking paints. There is usually a way of using any paint you want, even if it means completely removing all the old paint, but it is important to check the paint manufacturer's instructions. Do this yourself beforehand, even if you're having someone else do the work. House painting can be very expensive, and the wrong paint can waste a lot of money in a very short time. Moreover, the effects may not be apparent until some time after the job has been completed and the painter long gone.

THE INTERIOR

This book does not pretend to be a guide to interior decoration and all the techniques necessary to it, but an annual check of the paint or wallpaper on the interior walls, the finish on the woodwork, and the condition of the plasterwork is an important first step in keeping things looking their best.

Woodwork

Wood surfaces may be left untreated, or they may be stained, oiled, or otherwise sealed, and of course painted. Untreated surfaces, especially of lighter colored woods such as pine, can become dirty and shabby with time. Over a very long period (centuries), certain wood, like oak, can gradually obtain a much-appreciated patina, but in the short run it is likely that dirty surfaces will benefit from straightforward cleaning or perhaps a more permanent treatment such as painting.

Stained, oiled, or polyurethaned surfaces fare better and are less likely to need frequent refurbishing. Painted areas may need a more thorough inspection.

Interior Paint

When inspecting the condition of the paint on walls and ceilings, look also for signs of more serious damage, such as water stains, indicating a leaky roof, and badly cracked plaster, indicating foundation settling (see chapter 2). If repainting is necessary, it is best to plan it for early summer when windows and doors can be left open while the paint is drying.

Take special care in refinishing previously painted woodwork. Paint that is peeling badly or has otherwise deteriorated should probably be removed. Occasional blistered or peeling spots can be scraped free of loose paint, then leveled with patching compound. Finally, the entire surface should be lightly sanded, especially if the old paint was glossy, so that the new paint will adhere well. After you sand, be sure to remove all traces of dust, since paint will not adhere to dust either. One way to do this is with a tack cloth or a slightly dampened lint-free cloth.

Instead of sanding glossy surfaces, you can now apply one of several deglossing agents. These provide a "tooth" for the new paint. Some are toxic, however, and should be used with caution; all should be used strictly according to the directions. (See Ratings on interior and woodwork paints in the appendix.)

Plaster

In the last 40 years, the commonest form of interior wall covering has been *plasterboard,* a gypsum board often known by its most popular trade name, *Sheetrock*. But older houses were usually finished inside with solid plaster applied over wood or metal lathing. Solid plaster, when properly applied in a soundly constructed, well-kept house, will last a long time, especially if the plaster itself is also maintained by occasional painting or repapering. Although plaster is inherently strong, it can deteriorate as a result of damage to the rest of the house. Excessive moisture, whether caused by leaks or general dampness, can seriously harm plaster. Settling or movement of the house can also have a direct and deleterious affect on plastered surfaces. Insect damage or rot in a house's framework is a third threat.

Substantial plastering or replastering requires the skill of a professional and is a major undertaking. It is therefore important to understand what has caused any crumbling, cracking, bulging, or collapse that is evident. If the cause is structural movement, try to find out whether it has stopped and the house is now stable. If the plaster appears to have suffered water damage, make sure that the cause has been eliminated before adding good work to bad. If you suspect decay from rot or insect life, remedy the situation before starting any new work. In most of these cases, the plaster will have to be removed to cure the underlying problem; it is a waste of time and money to plaster over problems that must be addressed later.

Unless you want to preserve the plaster for architectural authenticity or for some unique textured surface, plasterboard is very nearly the equal of solid plaster in many respects and is decidedly easier and cheaper to apply. (If you use it as a base for wallpapering, no one will ever know what is underneath.) Furthermore, it is far easier to apply paint to plasterboard than to plaster. Although plaster is said by some to impart a more unified feeling of strength to a house, plasterboard actually has more resistance to racking forces and is therefore considered a better interior wall treatment for houses in earthquake-prone areas.

Check the condition of any gypsum wallboard. If it is in good shape, you may be hard-pressed to identify it as such; but if the job has been done badly, there are a number of faults that may be evident. Insufficient support and poor nailing can result in bowing and sagging of sections and popping of nails. Nails that have been insufficiently set or filled can cause rust stains to appear through the finish. Trauma-type damage can leave areas that need replacing or patching. Practically all the above have only one cure: removal and reinstallation by more qualified workers. Once properly installed, gypsum wallboard requires little maintenance other than the periodic painting or wallpapering that is common to other interior wall surfaces.

Wallpaper

Any inspection of a house's cosmetics involves assessing the condition of the wallpaper. Apart from normal wear and tear, the common faults with wallpapered areas—loose sections, stains, and discoloration—are generally the result of improper application. If walls were not properly sized and sealed and otherwise appropriately prepared, the wallpaper will not remain in pristine condition for very long. However, sometimes the fault is more serious, the result of an underlying problem, such as settling or excessive moisture. Again, these conditions must be solved before repapering is done.

FIVE

Summer Preparation

As winter recedes, the outside will begin to claim more of your time. Gardeners can remove the mulch from snowdrops and crocuses and prune their fruit trees. Trellises should be repaired and painted, if necessary, before they begin to be covered by vines and climbing plants, and a general cleanup can be undertaken of broken branches, items buried under the snow, and other debris.

Those who are not horticulturally inclined can look forward to enjoying the terrace, the garden, and even the pool if there is one. These areas need some attention too, however. Now is the time to make a checklist of garden furniture, accessories, and other installations—outdoor lights, barbecues, hot tubs, swimming pools—and have them serviced or refurbished as necessary. Don't wait until the day before guests are to arrive.

PORCHES, VERANDAS, AND DECKS

Halfway between the outside and the inside are a variety of structures—enclosed or semienclosed porches, verandas, decks, balconies, and even widow's walks (small rooftop decks). Many of these are subject to the stresses of weather. It is hard to lay down any universal rule for their inspection, since their size and construction can vary so much. Nevertheless, look over such structures on a regular basis as part of your summer preparation.

Wood flooring, whether on an older porch or newer deck, is probably the element that deserves the closest attention. Check the condition of the basic structure—is it still firm and free from rot or deterioration?—and the condition of its finish—does it need restaining or repainting?

Inspection and Repair of Wooden Decking

Restaining or, more usefully, retreating with a preservative (which may or may not also stain) is best done on clean, dry wood. It should go without saying that the condition of all areas to be treated should be checked to ensure that there is no rot and no damaged or missing boards.

Start your inspection by making sure that all nails in the decking are set below the surface—they can sometimes work up as the result of boards giving when they are walked on, and then pose hazards. If a nail refuses to stay set, replace it with a ringed or annular nail, preferably one that is galvanized. Nongalvanized nails may rust and stain the surrounding areas, especially if they are left unpainted and are not stained or treated along with the rest of the deck.

Sometimes not only nails will have popped up above the surface but entire boards may have warped or bowed. These should be either turned over or replaced with new, flat boards. Similarly, any section or length that displays signs of structural deterioration should be replaced. Whether replacing a board or merely turning it over, avoid using the same nail holes. If this is impossible, replace the nails with screws somewhat larger than the nailholes. Any areas that need to be replaced because of rot should be treated with wood preservative to prevent a recurrence of the condition. When replacing boards, be sure to use material that is the same size as the original—uneven floors are as dangerous as unsound floors.

After checking all the floor areas, turn your attention to rails and supports. These are very often fixed with bolts that can be easily retightened with a wrench or screwdriver. Sagging joists or stair framework can often be reinforced simply by attaching another wooden member, the same size as the original, to the weakened part, taking care to jack up the first member to its proper position before attaching the support.

Other wooden constructions around the grounds, such as gates and fences, should be checked for continued sturdiness and possible deterioration. If fences are sagging, it may be necessary to replace the fence posts. Set the new ones at least 18 inches below ground level and perhaps embed them in already-mixed concrete. This is also the time to oil and repaint all hinges, latches, and other hardware on gates, large and small.

Stairs and steps—especially the hand and guard rails—should also be inspected to assure yourself that they have not been weakened during the winter.

If a porch or veranda has been wholly or partly enclosed with either windows or screens, these should be included in the window inspection discussed in the following section.

WINDOWS

Recently constructed houses are built with window units that comprise built-in screens and energy-efficient double-glazing. Many older houses have been retrofitted with triple-track storm-and-screen combinations. Most older houses, however, still rely on a system of removable storm and screen windows that are exchanged for each other at the beginning and end of the winter. Taking these screen and storm windows in and out every year exacts a toll on them. Since their efficiency is largely governed by how well they fit, check that they are in good repair. Even if you don't have to deal with this chore, you should still inspect all the windows at this time. Be sure they operate easily, so you'll be able to open and close them readily when summer comes, and also check the condition of the glazing and the integrity of the screens.

Glass

The glass in the windows should be well fitted in the sash and have no cracks. It is annoying to have to replace a large pane of glass because of a small crack in one corner, but even that crack can cause heat to escape. It may be possible to run a small bead of clear epoxy glue over the crack, but replacement is best. (Besides, the damaged pane can always be recut to fit a smaller frame somewhere else.)

The glass is set in the frame, properly called the sash, either with old-fashioned putty (fast disappearing because of its poisonous lead content) or with synthetic glazing compounds. The latter have the advantage of staying soft so they won't crack and fall out so quickly.

FIGURE 5.1 *Crack in glass*

However, even glazing compound is not permanent and will eventually deteriorate. When sections do crack and fall out, the window should be reglazed. Water will work its way into the frame, and it will rot (if made of wood) or rust (if made of metal). In either case the window will become drafty and energy-inefficient. The reglazing operation is easy and will prolong the life of the sash, to say nothing of your sense of satisfaction when you observe a winter storm beating on the secured glass.

Here's how to do it: First, remove all the remaining putty or glazing compound. If the pane is broken, you can break it even more, then carefully remove the remaining shards. This facilitates the removal of the glazing compound. If the compound has become very hard, it sometimes helps to apply a little heat, carefully, to soften it. The easiest way to do this is with a small propane torch. A special flaring nozzle can be obtained at most hardware stores, which will direct a shaped flame, particularly suitable for aiming at putty or other forms of glazing compound. Adjust the flame to about 2 inches in length, and hold the torch so that the tip of the flame barely touches the area to be softened. Test frequently with a spackle knife to see how quickly the material is responding. Take care not to burn any adjacent woodwork. If you are merely going to apply fresh glazing compound and intend to reuse the pane, be more careful removing the old compound. In either case, remove the little metal pins or clips (called *glazing points*) that hold the glass in the wood sash.

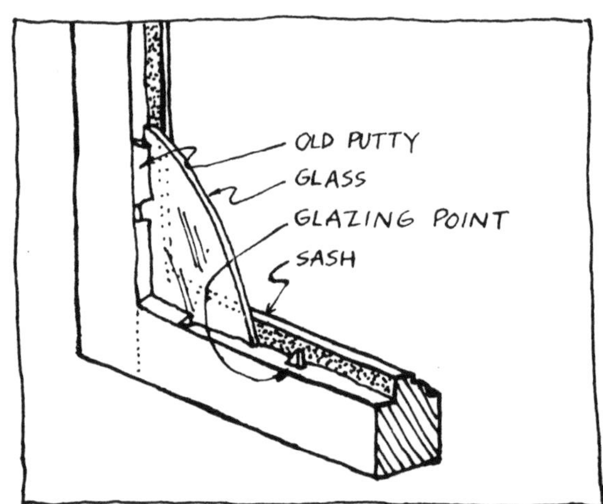

FIGURE 5.2
Glazing points and sash anatomy

With a chisel, scrape clean the recess (called the *rabbet*) in the sash where the glass fits. Ideally, the rabbet should now be painted. Unpainted rabbets in wood sash should be given a coat of linseed oil, especially if putty is going to be used. Now a thin bead of putty or compound should be laid in the rabbet. This step is often skipped; as a result, the glass may not seat tightly against the rabbet in the sash and so allows moisture—which may condense on the inside of the window—to run down between glass and sash, causing a premature deterioration in the glazing.

Now install the pane of glass, which has been cut to exact measure, and seat it firmly against the bead of compound in the rabbet. There

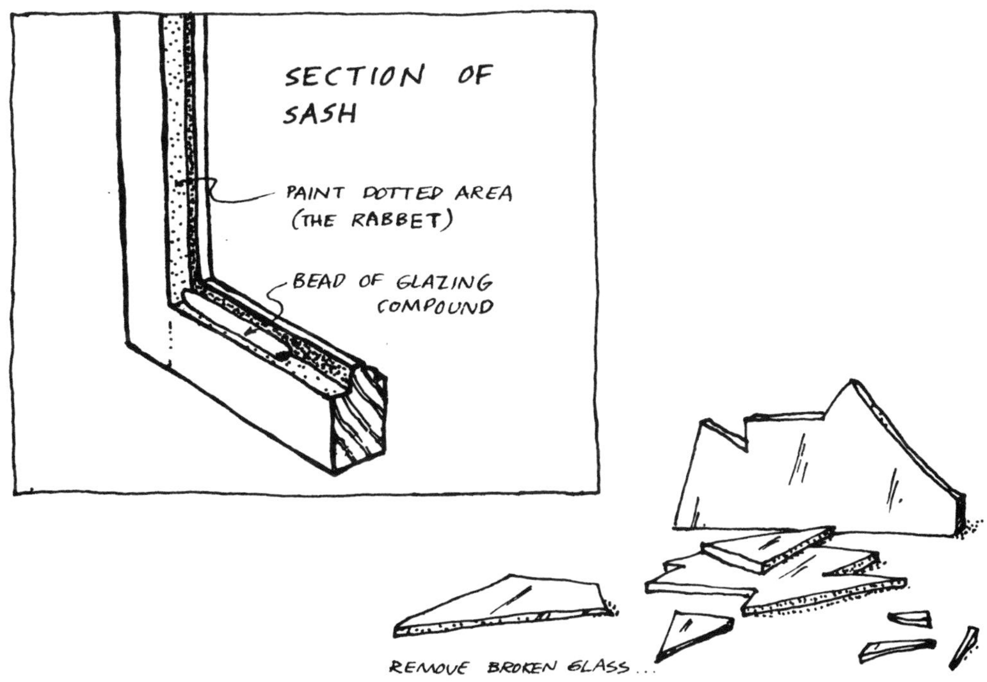

FIGURE 5.3 *Preparing sash for reglazing*

should be no gaps and no rattles. Secure it in place with glazing points pushed in every 10 inches or so. The lipped type (see figure 5.4) are the easiest to insert. Place the points so they hold the glass tightly, but not so tightly that the glass is inadvertently cracked. (Laying a thin bead of compound in the rabbet first makes proper seating much easier.)

Roll the glazing compound back and forth between your hands to make it soft and pliable. Press a thin roll of it against the glass, then smooth it out by pressing firmly with a putty knife drawn at an angle along the rabbet.

FIGURE 5.4 *Inserting glazing points*

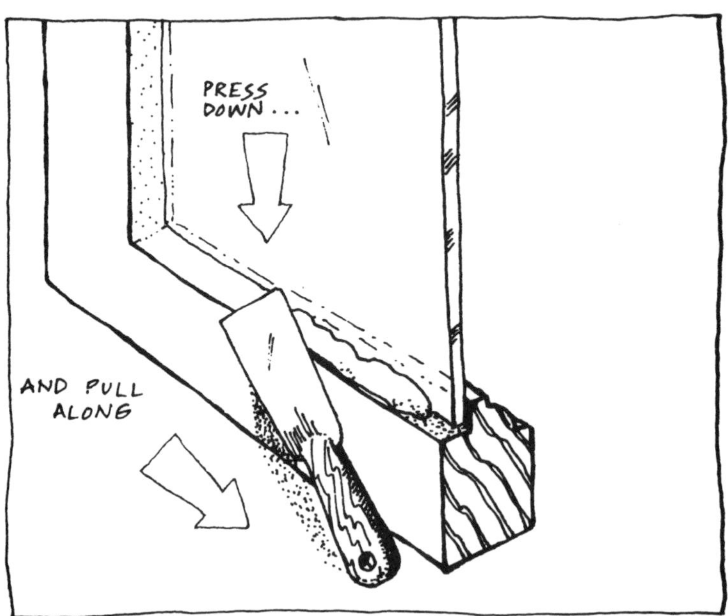

FIGURE 5.5 *Applying glazing compound*

The new compound must be painted, but wait a week before doing so to let the compound dry. If you don't wait, the paint may pull the compound out; and if you don't paint, the compound will eventually dry completely and fall out of its own accord.

When checking the condition of the glazing, also check that the paint is generally adhering well to the windows and their frames and not peeling or blistering, and that there is no rot anywhere.

Screens

As the weather turns warmer, you'll want to open the windows to ventilate your house. In most areas, you'll need screens to do so comfortably.

If you have removable screens and storm windows, make sure, as you replace each set, that they are key-numbered to the window on which they belong. There are numbered pins sold just for this purpose.

FIGURE 5.6 *Numbering removable storm windows*

Before you put up the screens, look them over carefully for tears or holes; these are easier to repair before the screens are installed. Sometimes what may at first glance appear to be a small hole in wire screening is actually just the mesh spread apart. Use a nail or some other sharp object to realign the wires. Real tears can be repaired by gluing or weaving.

If you repair nylon-mesh screens with a glued-on patch, epoxy is a good glue to use, but even shellac will work (see figure 5.7). For a more permanent job on wire-mesh screens, the weaving method (see figure 5.8) is best.

Of course, both glued and woven patches will be evident, and if the tear is large and appearances are very important, the only solution is to replace the whole screen wire.

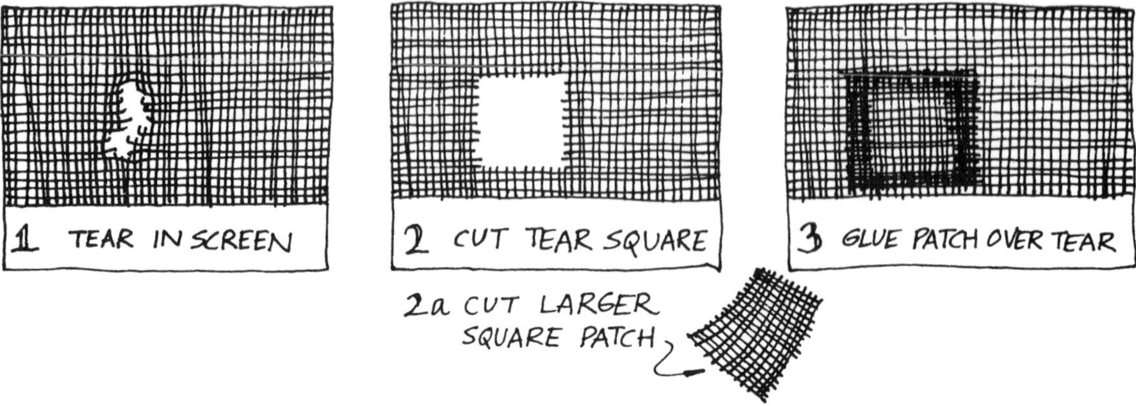

FIGURE 5.7 *Glued patches*

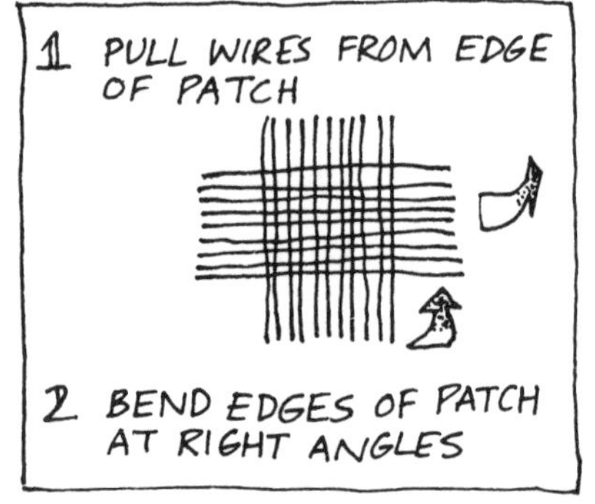

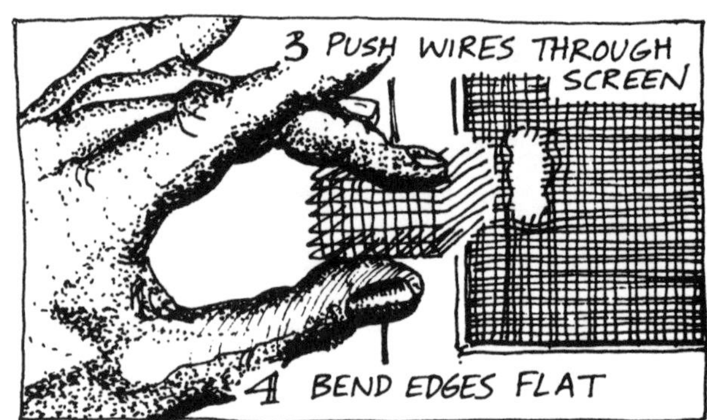

FIGURE 5.8 *Woven patches*

ROOF AND ATTIC AREAS

After winter's cold is past and before the heat of summer arrives is the best time to take a look at the area under the roof. Most houses have some accessible space between the ceiling of the highest room and the roof. In some houses, the height is very restricted; in others, the attic is a large stand-up space. Large or small, the space is typically uninsulated and consequently can become very cold in winter and very hot in summer.

Leaks

The first thing to look for is signs of leaking. Any water stain should be viewed with suspicion; reinspect during a steady rain to determine whether it is an old (and presumably repaired) leak or a current problem. See chapter 2 for a discussion on how to locate the origin and cause of roof leaks.

Ventilation

Assuming that the area (whether full attic or tiny crawl space) is dry, the next thing to check is whether it is well ventilated, to prevent the potentially damaging effects of condensation. Usually an attic is built with louvered vents in the gables at each end of the building so that there is sufficient flow-through ventilation.

The best time to check the efficiency of the ventilating system is on a sunny but cold day, with the temperature down around freezing. If the underside of the roof facing away from the sun is damp or wet, there is not enough ventilation. The moisture in the attic is condensing on the cold underside of the roof. In that case, install more openings, or possibly add an exhaust fan to push the air through more efficiently. Of course, if the heated area of the house is properly

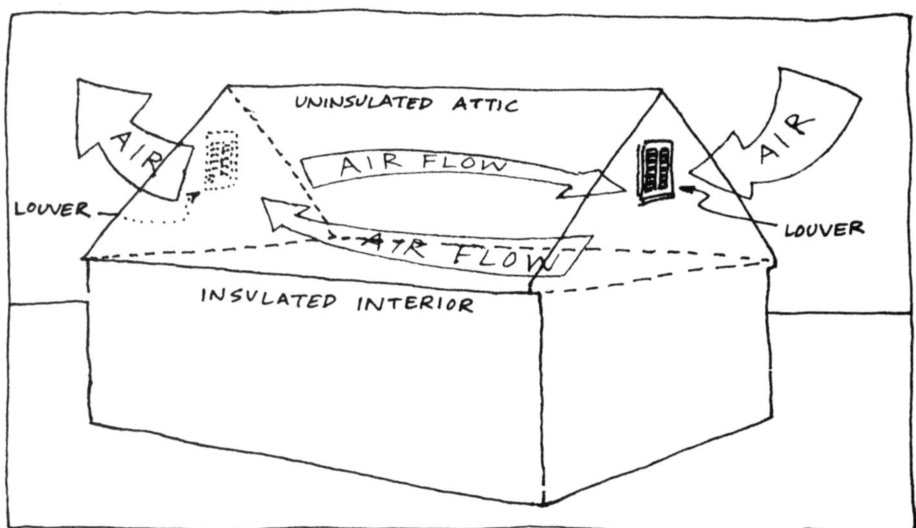

FIGURE 5.9 *Roof ventilation*

enclosed with vapor barriers (see chapter 9), there shouldn't be much moisture in the attic to condense—but if there is, more ventilation will help.

Note that ventilation openings in the gable, even if louvered, will attract unwanted tenants such as birds, bats, rodents, and insects. The vents therefore should be screened, and the screening checked once a year. See that it has not torn, allowing animals in, or become so clogged with leaves or other debris that no air can pass through. Brush the screen clean and patch any holes, if necessary, or replace it if this is easier.

Insulation

While you are in the attic checking the ventilation, make sure that the insulation in the floor is in good condition. If you have loose insulation (such as poured vermiculite) between the ceiling joists of the room below, see that it still forms a continuous barrier. Sometimes rodents chew away tunnels and build nests here, creating spaces for heat to leak out. If this has happened, replace the missing insulation or simply rearrange what is there to fill the spaces. (You might also set some traps.)

FIGURE 5.10 ***Rodent activity in attic insulation***

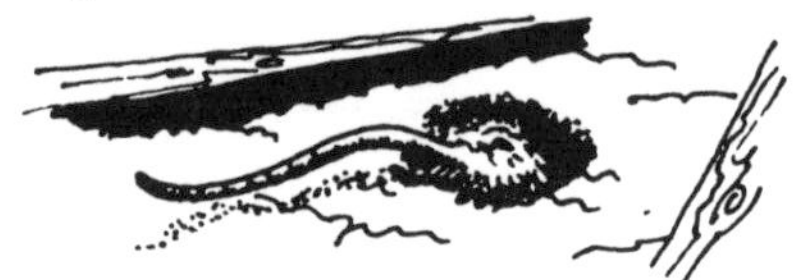

PROTECTION AGAINST LIGHTNING

Thunderstorms are most likely to occur in summer, so some thought should be given at this time to protection against lightning. Lightning is the result of large quantities of positive (or negative) electrical charges building up in storm clouds and being attracted to an equal quantity of negative (or positive) charges in the ground below. When the attraction becomes great enough, the gap is suddenly bridged, releasing millions of volts and thousands of amperes. Nearby air molecules are heated up and explode, resulting in the noise we call thunder.

The important thing to bear in mind is that the bridging effect takes place at the point where the two charges can get closest to each other, that is, from the storm clouds to tops of the tallest objects in the area—trees, poles, masts of ships, or, what concerns us here, houses.

FIGURE 5.11
Lightning path

The damage that can result from this sudden passage of enormous energy is caused by the resistance of the path taken by the "spark." For example, wood is not a very good conductor of electricity and so can be badly damaged when resisting it. Copper rods or wires, on the other hand, are good conductors of electricity; they offer little resistance and suffer minimal damage.

Therefore, if your house stands out in an open area, it should be protected from a possible lightning strike by a system of terminals or rods which, projecting above the roof, are connected by heavy cables to one another and then to equally thick wires leading to metal plates, rods, or pipes buried deep in the ground.

For maximum protection and insurance benefits, such a system should be installed by professionals and supplied with a Master Label plate certifying that sufficient Underwriters' Laboratory-approved rods, conductors, and grounds have been satisfactorily installed.

Not only the house but television and radio antennas, water pipes, waste pipes, and wiring systems should be equipped with suitable lightning arresters. If you have a treasured ornamental tree that is both tall and exposed, it too should be protected by lightning rods—the cost is small compared with the years required to grow it. The

FIGURE 5.12 *Lightning rods*

maintenance of these systems consists of making sure that all the constituent parts are still in place and connected.

PROTECTION AGAINST PESTS

We've already discussed the rodents that sometimes inhabit attic insulation, but there are various other creatures, large and small, that may invade your house from time to time. Such invasions include termites, carpenter ants, and wood-boring beetles, which should be eradicated as swiftly as possible (see chapter 2). However, certain other creatures deserve a little more consideration, for they may actually be useful. A couple of bats in the attic, for example, help keep the wasps under control. And wasps in moderation are not all bad, since they help keep the number of spiders down. Spiders in turn are useful in reducing the fly population. Since in practice it is very difficult to secure a house completely against every invader, a balanced population is actually to be encouraged.

Cats—unless you overfeed or restrain them—can generally be relied on to keep the rats and mice away. If you live in the country, a dog will keep the raccoons out of your chicken house and away from your garbage cans. Deer and rabbits in your garden can be kept out only by tall fences, which also should extend somewhat underground to thwart burrowing.

Skunks and porcupines, which occasionally take up residence underneath houses (porcupines especially like to chew away porch supports), are best caught in humane traps and removed to another neighborhood. Don't let your dog attempt to drive either off the property, or you'll end up with a foul-smelling or a spiky dog.

If you find silverfish, cockroaches, millipedes, and salamanders appearing in cupboards and closets, your house probably is too damp. Air it all out, improve the general ventilation, and keep all the hidden spaces scrupulously clean. Such efforts are much better than poisoning your house with insecticide.

FIGURE 5.13 *Bats in the attic*

It is said that no matter how much you clean there will always be at least one spider in every bedroom. One may be fine, especially if it is discreet, but sometimes even the most innocuous insects arrive in droves (or swarms or packs or whatever). Try to identify the newcomers before you take action.

Ladybugs (or ladybirds as they are called in England), which often hibernate under shingles, sometimes come out to bask in a warm winter's sun, and their numbers can be staggering. But don't rush for

FIGURE 5.14 *The aphid*

the exterminator; they are our best allies in combating that pernicious garden menace—the aphid.

Elm-leaf beetles, on the other hand, which also are wont to make sudden appearances inside and outside en masse in the fall, should be swept up and eliminated. They do little that is good and help carry the fungal disease that has destroyed elm trees across the nation.

A clean, well-ventilated house with well-screened windows is your best protection against unwanted visitors. Specific deterrents and remedies are as legion as the pests they are designed for. The most important rule is not to go overboard in combating one particular enemy, for everything in nature is interconnected, and you cannot remove one link without affecting the remainder—often producing a worse problem than you had at first.

SIX

Keeping Cool

Summer can be uncomfortably hot in many parts of the United States. To keep cool, we have come to rely on energy-expensive equipment. We often spend as much to cool our houses in summer as to heat them in winter. Buildings can be redesigned to take advantage of natural methods, from timed solar shading and proper orientation to once common methods such as high ceilings, inner courtyards, and greater use of shaded porches and outside walkways.

We suggest a dual approach to the problem of keeping cool: First, look for ways to improve the general situation—to lower the temperature or improve ventilation. Second, make sure that your cooling equipment is regularly maintained so it operates at maximum efficiency.

IMPROVING THE SITUATION

There are several things you can do to keep your surroundings cooler in the summer without necessarily increasing your energy bill. These include adding to the insulation, improving the ventilation, and increasing your protection from direct sunlight.

Insulation

The chief purpose of insulation is to reduce heat transference, whether from the inside out or from the outside in. Hence most of the discussion in chapter 8 concerning insulation applies as much to keeping cool as to keeping warm. Whatever improvements you can make to the insulation of the house will help lower cooling as well as heating bills.

Ventilation

You may be fortunate enough to live in a house where the design of the floor plan and the layout of the windows permit abundant cross-ventilation. Strategic opening of windows in various rooms can increase the flow of air and cut down the buildup of heat. To do this comfortably, of course, requires screens in good condition (see chapter 5).

Even without natural cross-ventilation, you can do a great deal to remain comfortable by using fans. Properly placed and well-maintained fans can be very efficient in terms of energy consumption—and their running cost is only a fraction of that for an air conditioner. They are usually quieter and can prevent the hermetic claustrophobia sometimes associated with air-conditioning. Their location should be arranged so that the maximum amount of air is moved through the room or building in as unobstructed a path as possible.

Floor fans are of course more easily arranged to direct air through any given series of rooms than window fans, although they may not always be as efficient in actually forcing the warm interior air to the outside.

Not all fans are created equal; some are larger than others, and some run at different speeds. For optimum efficiency, employ a fan geared toward your particular living space, preferably one that is adjustable according to varying temperatures and ambient conditions. For example, the use of a fan that may be turned to a slower speed at nighttime—when the air often cools—results in substantial savings over a period of time. Furthermore, despite modern advances in technology, many fans are irritatingly noisy, especially to the light sleeper. To be able to reduce the noise by slowing the speed can be a godsend to such individuals.

Shades and Awnings

Houses that are designed to take advantage of alternative energy systems frequently make use of automatic or semiautomatic window-shading devices, timed to take advantage of the free heat the sun can provide and at the same time maintain a comfortable ambient temperature in the house. Only a few newer houses are so cleverly designed, however. Nevertheless, even a nineteenth-century farmhouse can be kept surprisingly cooler than otherwise with the appropriate use of blinds and shades.

Although blinds and shades may be used inside to keep the sun out, it is far more efficient to keep the sun from striking the windows in the first place. Awnings on the outside can do precisely that. They can be adjustable, although fixed awnings, depending on the material used, may create interesting adjuncts, such as porches and covered decks. Note that an awning should not trap hot air against the house—there should be space for air to flow up behind it.

MAINTENANCE OF COOLING EQUIPMENT

Like other equipment in the house, the appliances involved in climate control require periodic inspection and occasional servicing.

Air Conditioners

Houses are air-conditioned either by individual room units or by a central system. If you have a central system, it is wise to have it professionally serviced once a year. Such a service should include checking the refrigerant level (and for leaks) and the internal operating pressures, making sure all belts are in good condition and properly adjusted, lubricating wherever necessary, and thoroughly cleaning (and replacing where necessary) the fins, filters, coils, and other areas in which dirt and debris may accumulate.

Apart from professional servicing, there are a couple of things that you can attend to yourself: inspect the filter—on a monthly basis when the unit is operating—and wash or replace it as necessary; keep the grills and registers unobstructed and lint-free by dusting or vacuuming occasionally.

Individual room units are rarely seen by a professional until they break down. It is therefore important that you keep an eye on them if they are to remain trouble-free for as long as possible.

The newer the unit, the less attention it should need, since moving parts are often sealed and lubricated for life. In addition, the condensate (often a source of trouble in earlier models) is now evaporated by small built-in heaters rather than being allowed to drain away outside. Nevertheless, filters should still be kept clean by washing or replacement, according to the type used.

If the unit is an older model, follow the procedures outlined in the owner's manual regarding lubrication and cleaning. If you have no manual, carefully brush or vacuum dust and lint from grilles, coils, and fan blades from time to time. This will ensure optimum air flow and go a long way toward keeping the air conditioner operating at maximum efficiency. Cleaning should be done from both the inside and the outside, although it is sometimes easier to bring the entire unit into the room to do this task, especially if it is mounted through the wall rather than through a window. Unplug the unit first in any case. Make sure that drain pans and outlets are clean and unobstructed; that will reduce the possibility of rusting. If you find any rust, clean it away with steel wool and touch up the spot with special rustproofing paint.

Finally, inspect the installation of the unit to confirm that it is secure and airtight. Wall-mounted units are generally set into sleeves that are built into the wall. The sleeve should be caulked where it passes through the wall, and the unit itself should be adequately weatherstripped so that it fits snugly into the sleeve. Seams and joints around a window-mounted unit, and the expansion slide that fits it to the window, should be caulked or fitted with foam weatherstripping.

Fans

Once you start counting, you may be surprised by the number of fans in your house. Not all of them are related to summer cooling, yet all can be profitably inspected at this time.

1. Kitchen exhaust fans, usually found in hoods but sometimes mounted separately in the wall or ceiling near the stove, have filters that must be kept clean if the fan is to be effective. If the kitchen seems to hold the steam and fumes, even when the fan is running, take out the screen or filter. Since the problem almost always involves the buildup of grease, it is best to remove the filter completely and wash it in hot water and detergent.
2. Attic-ventilating fans and bathroom fans are closely related—their job is to remove hot, moist air to the outside. Whereas bathroom fans are usually wired into the light switch so that they operate whenever the light is turned on (usually whenever the bathroom is used—it being the lack of a window that necessitates both artificial light and forced ventilation), attic fans are generally wired to a thermostat that restricts the operation of the fan to certain preset temperature limits. Wiring problems can be common to both and usually require the help of a qualified electrician, but it is worthwhile to make the following preliminary investigations yourself. Check to see whether there are any loose, frayed, or disconnected wires, that the fan blades are tightly connected to their hub, and that none of the blades is bent or twisted. After disconnecting the power supply to the fan, any loose or frayed wires are usually easily repaired. Fixing bent, loose, jammed, or missing fan blades can dramatically improve the operation of the fan, making it quiet and vibrationless again.
3. Many fans are also equipped with safety screens, fences, or guards. Inspect them to make sure that they are still securely attached and not bent or otherwise obstructing the operation of the fan.
4. Most fans require a drop of oil on the bearings once in a while, or they may squeak, run slowly, or ultimately not run at all.

Dehumidifiers and Air-Circulating Systems

Dehumidifiers are usually relatively small portable units that require only an occasional cleaning and inspection to make sure that they are not rusting or leaking.

Forced warm-air heating systems sometimes give you the option of running the blower unit without the furnace being operated. This is known as continuous air circulation, or CAC. It allows you to use the heating-duct system to recirculate air throughout the house, which can be an advantage during the summer—it provides some air movement and equalizes the temperature. The blower unit is usually operated by a separate switch from the one used to turn the furnace on and off; it should be clearly marked. Such a system requires that the furnace air filter be inspected on a regular basis during the summer as well as during the winter, and that all vents, registers, and grilles be kept open and clean.

PART II

Fall and Winter

SEVEN

Cold Weather Preparation

The keen gardener is probably more aware of the passing of summer than the rest of us, who wake up with surprise some frosty morning to note that summer is gone and fall is here. Although the gardener will have been making preparations for some time, the prudent homeowner—even if not a gardener—will find plenty of necessary things to do.

As the leaves fall, you may not worry about raking them off the lawn, but you should make sure that a few key areas start the winter relatively leaf-free. Keeping such places clear protects against drainage problems that can develop whether you live in snow country or in warmer areas, where winter is characterized as the rainy season.

ROOF DRAINAGE SYSTEM

Buildup of Leaves

Leaves can fall into gutters and downspouts and accumulate in the valley—the junction between two roof slopes. The buildup of leaves will prevent proper and complete drainage and should be cleaned out.

If trees overhang the roof, take extra precautions to ensure that no

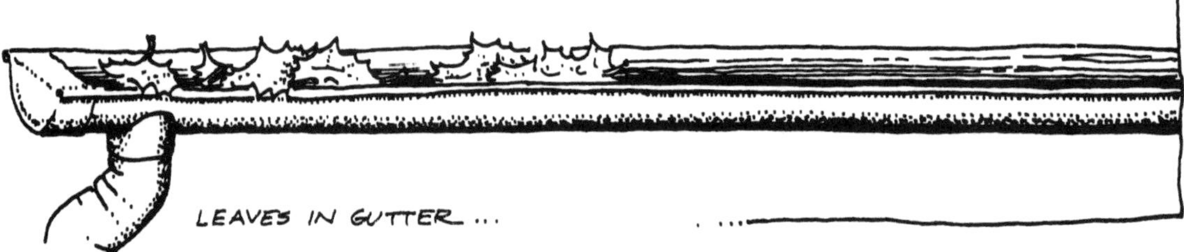

FIGURE 7.1 *Where leaves collect*

dead leaves accumulate in the valleys or elsewhere. Needle-bearing trees such as pine, hemlock, and redwood can be just as much a nuisance in this respect as broad-leaved trees. Clogged gutters can lead to a special winter problem—ice dams.

Ice Dams

A long period of freezing weather makes for great ice-skating but unfortunately can also lead to problems with the roof if a heavy snow falls.

Sunny weather after the snowfall can melt some of the snow on the roof, but if the temperature has remained around freezing the melted snow quickly forms icicles at the edge of the roof. This may look pretty but can be a harbinger of serious drainage problems.

As the thaw-and-freeze cycle continues, the icicles grow and begin to form a wall of ice along the roof edge. This creates an ice dam, which holds back the water that would otherwise run off the roof. As it backs up behind the dam, the water begins to seep back under the shingles and down into the house.

The main cause of an ice dam is an uninsulated or insufficiently

FIGURE 7.2 *Icicles at roof edge*

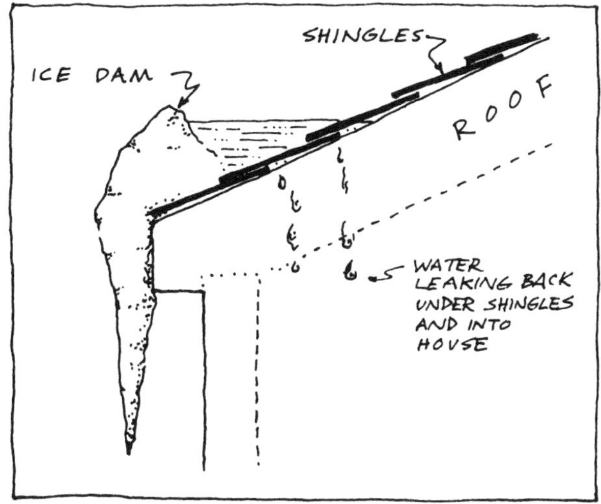

FIGURE 7.3 *Anatomy of an ice dam*

insulated roof. Heat from the interior of the house passes through the roof and melts the snow on it. The edge of the roof, however, which overhangs the outside wall, is not warmed in the same way; it retains its cover of frozen snow (and ice).

The first step in dealing with the problem is to make sure your roof is well insulated (see chapter 8). A well-insulated roof should keep most of its snow cover (since no heat is escaping through the roof to

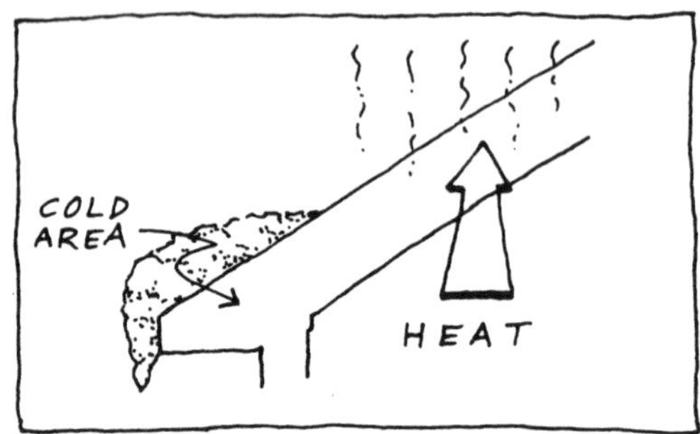

FIGURE 7.4 *Formation of an ice dam*

melt it); this in turn acts as additional insulation. In areas of heavy snowfall, of course, roofs are generally built with a steeper pitch (slope) so that heavy snows may slide off rather than overload the roof. Even so, some snow should still remain. If, soon after a snowfall, you can see patches of your roof through the snow cover, you can be pretty sure you're losing heat at those points.

FIGURE 7.5 *Uninsulated roof soon after a snowfall*

Another thing to check is that your gutters are not positioned to impede the runoff. While gutters should be placed to catch runoff of water, they ought to lie behind the slope of the roof (see figure 7.6). Otherwise they will catch snow that slides down the roof, which can then build up and possibly cause an ice dam. This is another reason that gutters should be kept cleaned out and free from obstructions such as dead leaves.

However, even if the roof is adequately pitched, the insulation sufficient, and the gutters properly positioned, ice dams may still occur. The only solution at this point is to install a heat tape along the bottom edge of the roof to prevent freezing and ice buildup.

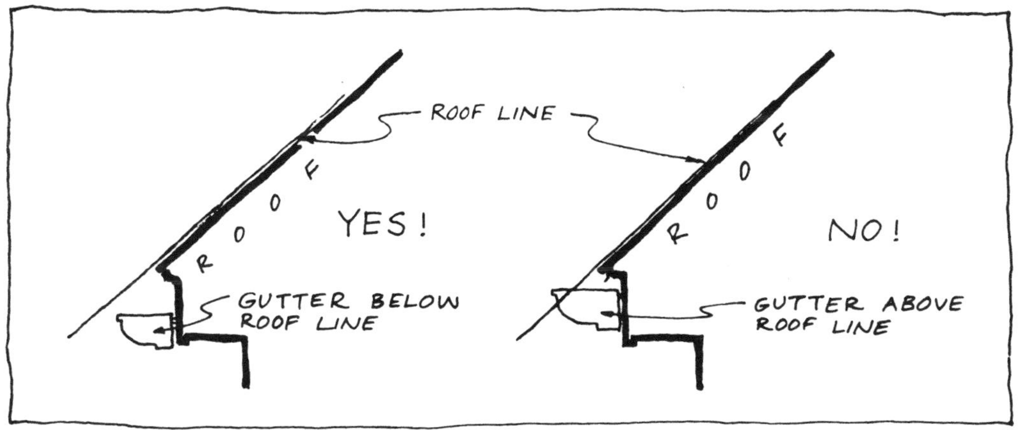

FIGURE 7.6 *Correct gutter alignment*

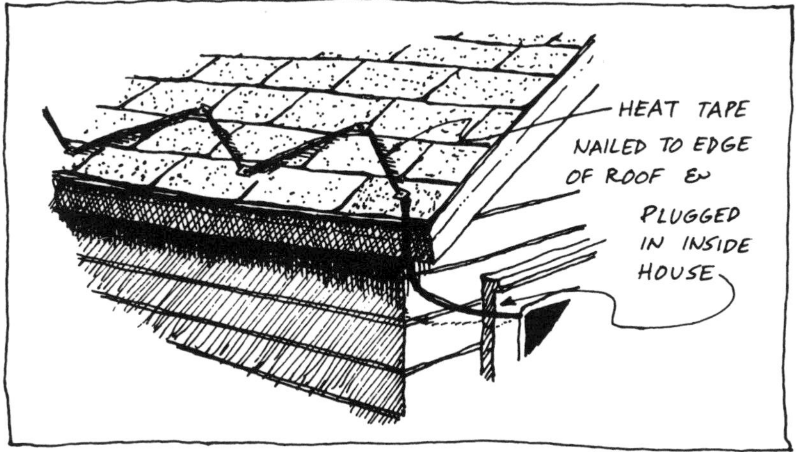

FIGURE 7.7 *Heat tape at roof edge*

Before the advent of efficient insulation and electric heat tape, the problem of ice dams was often solved in a practical but not particularly attractive way. The eaves were finished with a broad band of tin so that even if an ice dam did form there would be no shingles for trapped water to work back under. At the same time, projections were installed on the roof to hinder the snow from sliding off, since it formed useful insulation.

FIGURE 7.8 *Victorian house with tin eaves*

CULVERTS AND DITCHES

Leaves can also accumulate and clog up drainage ditches and culverts around the house and under the driveway. As soon as they are off the trees, the leaves seem to appear in the mouths of culverts, effectively blocking them. This may set the scene for a driveway-destroying flood or a lake of ice. Make the rounds with a long-handled shovel and be sure that all channels are clear. You may have to repeat the operation before the first snowfall.

FIGURE 7.9 *Clean culvert*

DRIVEWAYS

Now look at the driveway itself. Potholes may have begun to develop over the summer—they should be filled in now before the rain and snow and ice have a chance to turn them into deep pits.

If you live in an area where snowplowing is needed, delineate the driveway by stakes or fences to guide the snowplow as well as any visitors arriving by car. If you have lawns or flowerbeds lining the driveway, they can be hidden after a heavy snowfall—and be badly damaged by vehicles wandering into them.

FIGURE 7.10 *Marked driveway*

An equally important provision for the snowplow is a designated area where the mountains of plowed snow can be dumped. Unfortunately, the most convenient place often is an adjacent lawn. If you use the lawn this way and have a gravel driveway, when the snow finally melts you will be left with a large amount of gravel to rake back off the grass. Ideally the driveway should be large enough for one area of it to accommodate the plowed snow and still leave sufficient access.

FIGURE 7.11 *Snowbanks*

OVERHEAD WIRES

Another job that is best done when the trees are bare is to check that there are no overhead wires or equipment threatened by overhanging branches or dead trees at risk of falling. Inspect such items as

FIGURE 7.12 *A downed power line*

telephone lines, electric power lines and transformers, and radio and television equipment (antennas, cable connections, or satellite receiving dishes).

Power companies regularly patrol their lines along tree-lined roads, and you would be wise to follow suit for lines on your property. A fallen tree breaking a power line on a winter night can spell disaster. It is much easier to assess the problem on a fall day and then have dead trees and branches removed at your convenience.

While inspecting the various lines and other equipment, cast an eye on any utility poles you own to see that they are still sound and, if grounded, that the ground rods are still connected and firmly in the earth.

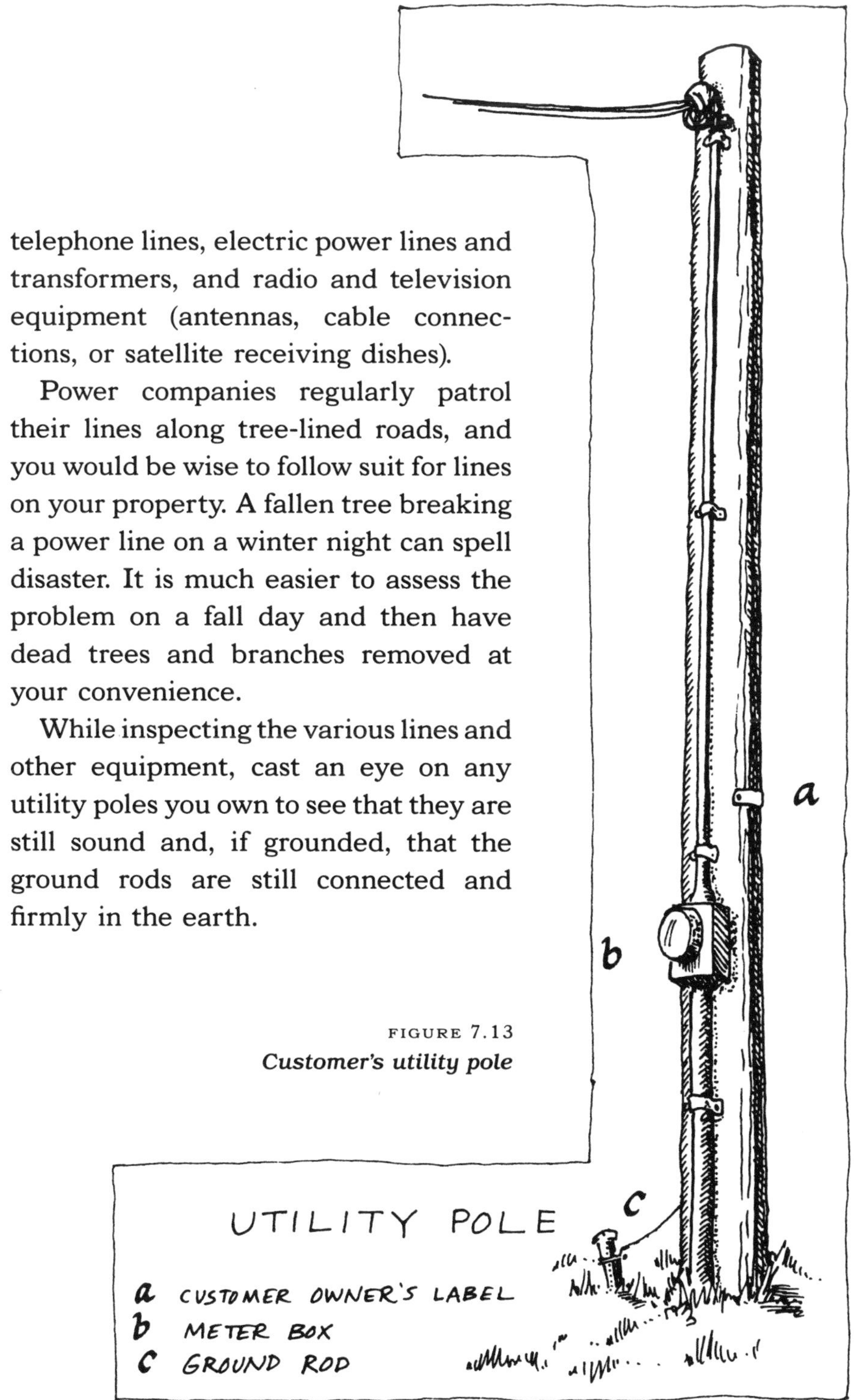

FIGURE 7.13
Customer's utility pole

EXTERIOR PLUMBING

If you live in an area that experiences freezing temperatures, you'll have to winterize all outside plumbing facilities. This can include entire installations such as swimming pools—which should be professionally serviced and prepared for winter at the end of the swimming season—and single items such as an outside faucet for a hose connection. Any kind of piping or plumbing connection must be either properly insulated or completely drained.

Such piping and plumbing connections can be insulated in one of two ways: by wrapping with insulation or enclosing in insulated boxes, conduits, or other containers, or by wrapping with thermostatically controlled heat tape, which is plugged in to the nearest electrical outlet.

Should either solution prove difficult or impossible, every section of the system that is in any way exposed—by being either outside or uninsulated under the house where there is no heat, for example—must be drained completely. This is possible only if there are shutoff valves in the system located at points still within the area not liable to freezing. Furthermore, for any section of plumbing to be capable of being drained, there must be no pockets of downslope such as U-shaped areas below and before the last drain point.

If you are not certain that any area has been completely drained, seek professional help to check levels and install any necessary shutoff valves.

STORAGE OF OUTDOOR EQUIPMENT

You may be surprised at how many things accumulate outside during the summer months. Garden furniture—including chaises, chairs, picnic tables, and umbrellas—barbecue and sports equipment, not to mention a host of garden tools and sundry other objects, all collect around even the smallest house with apparently no effort. If you don't deal with them in the fall, you'll discover them again in the spring—but rusted, rotted, or otherwise deteriorated past the point of utility.

Take the necessary steps now: overhaul, oil, and put away the garden tools—and then get out the snow shovels and snow blowers.

Retrieve, repair if needed, and safely store garden furniture, cookout materials, and sports equipment. If you cannot store it all indoors, it should at least be covered to protect it from the elements.

GROUNDS AND GARDEN

The last thing to check before the snow arrives is the condition of the grounds and garden. Ask yourself the following questions: Have all the spring bulbs been planted? Are all tender plants, such as roses, adequately protected by mulching? Have young evergreens been screened against drying winter winds? Have young fruit trees been surrounded with wire netting to keep out mice and rabbits?

FIGURE 7.14 *Protected shrubbery*

Rain barrels and large planters should be drained and turned upside down or covered to protect them from freezing and possibly cracking.

Vegetable gardens should be cleared of refuse and planted with a cover crop to protect the ground from leaching during the winter. Lawns should be cut at a height of 2 inches—any excess will die and form an impenetrable thatch that will make spring growth more difficult.

DISPOSING OF GARBAGE

As landfills become filled to capacity, it is becoming more important to exercise greater prudence and discretion in the way we dispose of our waste. In some localities it is already mandatory to sort and, where possible, recycle one's garbage. What this means for the average householder is the allotting of a little more organized space to accommodate the unending supply of used bags, bottles, and other waste material.

Now is a good time to plan and update these facilities to make sure that they are adequate. If, as is usually the case, they are outside the house, make sure that they are ready for winter. Keeping the actual garbage cans in bins can prevent animals from delving into the trash prior to its collection, but a heavy snowfall also may make the lids difficult for you to open. If there is the right kind of space, it would be better to keep the garbage cans against the side of the house on a platform with a small roof built over it.

FIGURE 7.15 *Garbage cans in summer and winter*

CHORES AFTER A SNOWFALL

Even those with small outdoor areas will find that there are chores to do from time to time during the winter. After a snowstorm, shake the snow with care from evergreen bushes and hedges to prevent the branches from breaking. Do this as soon as possible after the snow stops falling, before it has begun to harden and freeze. Be especially careful if it is very cold, for frozen branches are brittle and can easily be broken. At the same time, stamp the snow down firmly around fruit trees and other special trees to prevent rodents from tunneling in to feed off the bark. If you enjoy having birds around, feed them; they will especially appreciate feeding immediately after a storm. And if you stand your old Christmas tree upside down in the snow, you can provide some welcome extra shelter. However, if you do start feeding the birds, don't stop in midwinter, for they may have become dependent on you.

FIGURE 7.16 *Feeding the birds*

A FINAL TIP FOR WINTER

Ashes from a fireplace or stove, especially hardwood ashes, which are a very rich soil builder, can be used for garden compost. The ashes can also be used to make icy paths and steps safe. Commercially sold salt works better at melting ice—and ashes do become messy—but salt has a slowly disintegrating effect on concrete and cement. And it's hard on your pets' feet. So use salt sparingly.

EIGHT

Keeping Warm

You can keep warm at home by turning up the heat or putting on more clothes, or both. But for the greatest comfort and economy, it pays first to examine the component parts of the house to make sure each is contributing to the general efficiency of your heating system.

STORM DOORS AND WINDOWS

No matter how old your house is, and no matter how little or how much insulation is in the walls and roof, you can at least make sure that you're not losing heat through the doors and windows. Retrofitting doors and windows is an industry of its own; a complete set of storm doors and storm windows are guaranteed to keep you warmer and cut your heating bills.

If you already have a full set of storm windows and doors—whether permanently or seasonally installed—now is the time to make sure that all are in good order. Replaceable units especially should fit snugly within their openings.

Weatherstripping

The first step is to ensure that the storm doors and storm windows, together with the regular doors and windows, are draft-free.

Weatherstripping is your basic weapon here. It comes in many different forms, from common felt to springy metal strips and plastic tubing. The idea is to have a resilient material against the glass or frame to maintain the seal. The choice of material is not so important—the result should be a door or window that fits snugly in its opening.

For weatherstripping to achieve a maximum seal, it must be carefully installed. This is best done by trial-fitting the stripping before it is permanently attached. Check the fit with the door or window in both closed *and* open positions. Not all door and window openings remain square throughout their lives. When you install weatherstripping to an open unit, you may find on closing it that there is an unexpected (and unwanted) gap.

Tight fitting can go too far, however, and make a door or window hard or even impossible to open. Check that each does in fact open and close with relative ease.

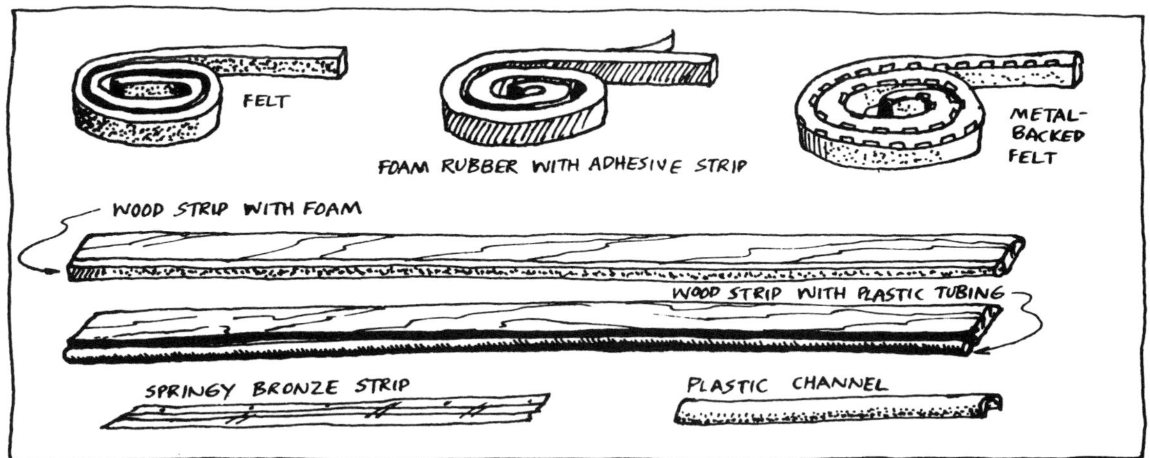

FIGURE 8.1 *Types of weatherstripping*

Other Problems with Fit

The problems may go beyond those that weatherstripping can solve. The hinges may be loose; tightening may be all that's required. The door or window, or its frame, may be swollen, warped, or out of alignment; fixing may require some real carpentry skills. Or succes-

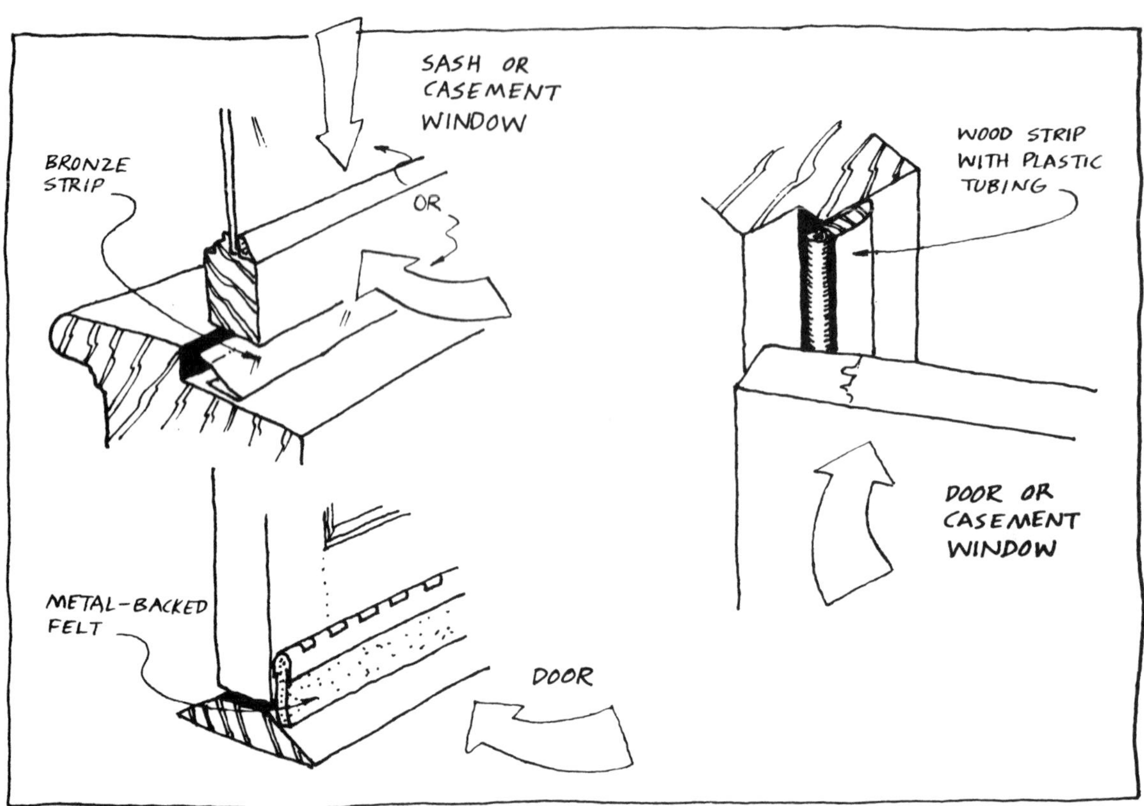

FIGURE 8.2 *Placement of weatherstripping*

sive paintings may have built up to an excessive thickness; scraping and removing this old paint is tedious but can be done.

Steel casement windows are especially vulnerable to fitting problems; without constant maintenance, they can easily rust. The rust builds up, making them difficult to open and, occasionally, impossible to close. They should be periodically cleaned and repainted, but, as with wood doors and windows, you cannot simply repaint forever. The time will come when some of the old paint has to be removed. Always use the proper rustproofing undercoat over the cleaned metal; otherwise, rust will begin again and the finish coat will deteriorate rapidly. (Aluminum frames need no primer and in fact are not usually painted.)

Sliding windows that are sticking should not present a great problem. Clean the dirt and grime out of the grooves in which they slide, and then lubricate the grooves by spraying them with silicone or by rubbing them with a bar of soap or a wax or paraffin candle.

FIGURE 8.3 *Lubricating a sliding window*

CAULKING

Defective caulking can contribute to the deterioration of exterior paint, but it is important in other ways, too. The many seams and joints in a house's exterior are all possible sources of heat leaks. For a house to be truly efficient in terms of heat conservation, all these openings must be tightly sealed. First-class carpentry and properly overlapping construction can eliminate certain openings; beyond that, the most effective way to close gaps is to fill them with some kind of caulking material.

If the gaps are large, however, they should be first filled with a fibrous packing material such as oakum, available at plumbing supply houses and hardware stores. But don't consider caulking as a quick and easy substitute for the proper repair and replacement of damaged sections of siding or door and window frames.

Many kinds of caulking material are now available. Each has its

FIGURE 8.4 *Places to caulk*

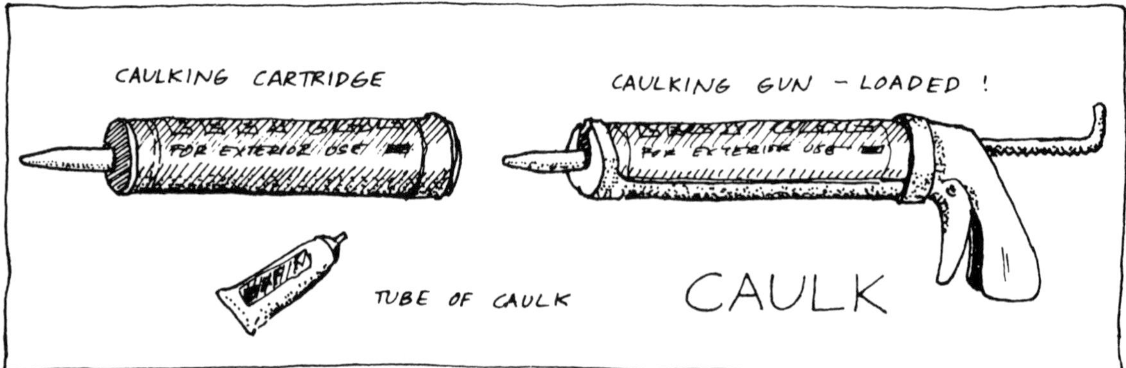

FIGURE 8.5 *Cartridge and tube caulk*

own unique characteristics and is designed to be used in specific places and for specific purposes. Nearly all of them are available in the familiar caulking cartridge used in a caulking gun. Some types, designed primarily for interior use, are supplied in smaller tubes.

Some popular types of caulking materials and their characteristics and applications are as follows:

1. *Oil-base caulking.* This type is the commonest and cheapest. Although it can be used for a variety of jobs, it suffers the drawback that it is not easily painted over. The problem is that

while it remains pliable, it will catch on any brush or foam applicator and possibly be pulled out of place. Furthermore, satisfactory coverage is not always achievable unless great care is taken to ensure that a compatible paint is used. This is usually not worth doing for the sake of the caulking; many other factors are more important in the choice of paint.

2. *Latex-base caulking.* This caulk dries fast but remains flexible, is good for many jobs, and can easily be painted over.
3. *Butyl rubber caulking.* Although more expensive than the first two types, butyl caulk lasts much longer and is very good for use in cracks between metal and masonry because it retains unusual flexibility.
4. *Polysulfide caulking.* An excellent, long-lasting material that adheres well to paint and to which paint itself adheres.
5. *Silicone caulking.* This type is the most expensive, but it also lasts the longest. However, many types of silicone caulking do not do well with paint, either over or under it. In fact, silicone is often intended for applications where paint is not involved, such as around bathroom tiles. It is available either clear or precolored.

Before you choose a type of caulking, consider what you intend to caulk and how it will be treated. Sometimes the exact type to use (as categorized above) is hard to determine, but the specific applications for any given caulk are invariably detailed on the product's label.

VENTS

Proper ventilation beneath the house is important (see chapter 2). Basement or crawl-space vents should be opened in preparation for summer. With the approach of winter, it is once again time to check these vents. Unless they are clear and operable (open and close easily), they are doing no good.

If the basement is unheated, and especially if there are water pipes running through it, it is a good idea to close these vents in late fall. As a further precaution, you can add some insulation, such as a piece of Styrofoam board cut neatly to shape on the inside, and perhaps a board on the outside to keep the snow out. Often basement vents are situated right below ground level, opening into a small well at the side of the house. In this case it helps to fill the pit with dead leaves. The leaves will provide a little extra insulation during the winter, and their removal in the spring affords an ideal opportunity to check the condition of these vents and ensure that they are opened for the summer.

FIGURE 8.6 *Basement vent*

Next, check the exhaust-fan vents. Typically installed in areas such as bathrooms and kitchens, these need cleaning from time to time. Some have removable filters that may be cleaned or replaced; others must be cleaned by hand. Check also that where the vent comes through the wall or roof to the outside there is a hood or cover sufficient to keep out wind, rain, and snow. Be sure the vent hood is well caulked (see preceding section).

Since gas heaters and gas water heaters must be vented to the outside, check that the pipes, thimbles, and hoods involved are all in good repair—well insulated where they pass through the wall and not rusted out anywhere. If the thimble, or sleeve through which the pipe makes its way to the outside, is deteriorating in any way, replace it. Don't try to repair it. The commonest variety, which comes in a range of sizes to fit different diameters of pipe, simply unscrews into two halves for removal (and screws together again for installation). One half is inserted through the wall from the inside, the other from the outside.

FIGURE 8.7 *Exhaust vent*

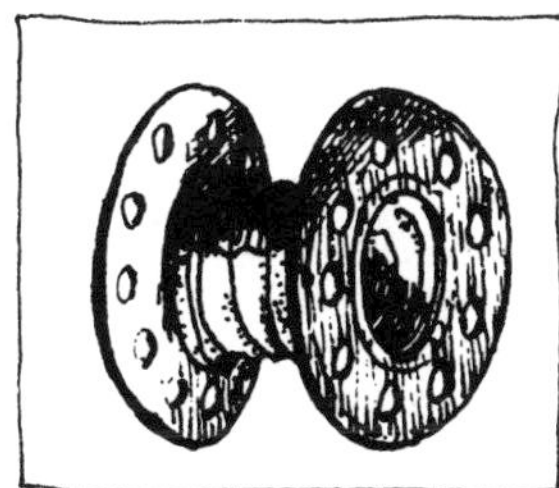

FIGURE 8.8 *Insulating thimble*

Some houses built in the last 30 years have eave vents. These are relatively small (1 to 2 inches in diameter) screened louvers inserted in the soffit, between rafters. They permit air to flow up behind the insulation into the roof and out through attic vents (see chapter 2) or, in some contemporary houses, through a continuous ridge vent at the roof peak.

The eave vents tend to get painted over, become blocked by wasps' nests, or sometimes just fall out. If your house has such vents, check that they are all present and firmly in place. Note, if you can, that the screens (designed to keep insects out of the attic) are still in place and in good condition.

Instead of small circular eave vents, whole sections of screened soffit—up to 2 feet in length—are sometimes employed to provide ventilation in this area; the same precautions and attention apply.

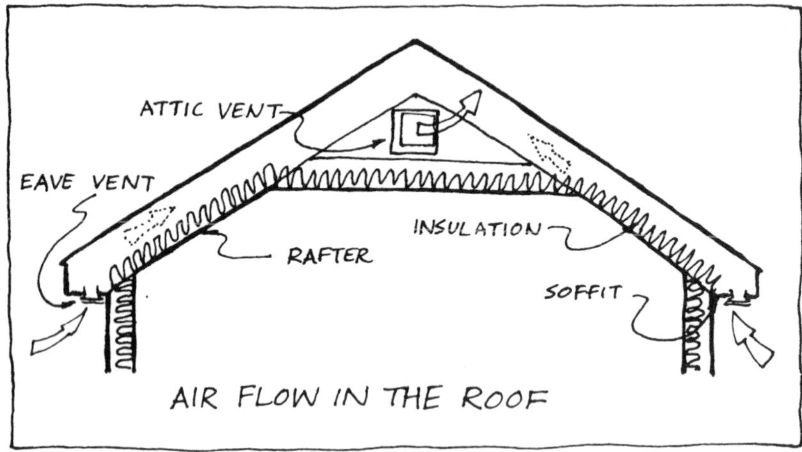

FIGURE 8.9 *Eave and attic vents*

Finally, usually high up in the gables are the attic vents (see chapter 5). A quick look now at the end of the summer can do no harm.

INSULATION

Although proper insulation should have been installed when your house was built, if you live in an older house there's a good chance it is underinsulated; it may even have no insulation at all. That's because building standards used to be quite different from what they are today. High energy costs now make it worthwhile to review the insulation in your house to determine whether it can be improved.

The purpose of insulation is to keep heat where it belongs—inside the house in cold weather and outside the house in hot weather. Today insulation is a virtual necessity if you consume energy for either heating *or* cooling.

Once you start dealing with insulation to maintain the temperature, you have to deal as well with humidity, which plays a large part in comfort control (see chapter 9). If you need insulation, then you also need a system of vapor barriers and ventilation.

If your house has little or no insulation, it will cost you more to leave it as is than to insulate it—increasingly so as energy costs rise. (Some local utility companies offer rebate incentives to their customers who undertake specific insulation programs.) Although measures such as storm windows, weatherstripping, and caulking are absolutely essential in any case and help considerably, they do not in themselves constitute a substitute for insulation. Fortunately, there are several kinds of insulation available that can either be added to already existing insulation, or started from scratch.

Most easily, you can insulate the attic, using loose-fill insulation material.

FIGURE 8.10 *Summer and winter insulation*

Loose-Fill Insulation

This type of insulation comes in large, light bags and is designed primarily for attic floors. You simply pour it between the attic joists that support the ceiling below. Loose-fill insulation is made from various materials such as ceramic fiber, glass wool, and vermiculite. Since some of these may contain hazardous materials, be careful to read labels and make sure that there is nothing harmful or toxic in the insulation you choose. Your choice should be based on the R-factor rather than on the price. The R-factor is the number assigned to the insulating qualities of any given material. The higher the number, the more efficient the insulation, regardless of its size and thickness. Common values considered acceptable are R-22 and above for ceilings and R-11 and above for walls. However, these values may vary according to the severity of the climate you live in and also according to the type of heat you use. Electric heat, for example, generally calls for a much higher R-factor than either hot-air or hot-water heat.

FIGURE 8.11 *Loose-fill insulation*

Blankets and Batts

Blankets and batts of insulation are the easiest forms of insulation to install in such places as the floors over unheated crawl spaces and basements, and the adjoining walls of unheated garages or other areas. Both are made in various widths (to fit between studs or joists spaced differently) and in different thicknesses (giving varying R-factors for different applications such as walls or floors). Batts are made in relatively short lengths, whereas blankets come in long rolls. Both can be obtained backed with either foil or some specially impregnated paper to provide a vapor barrier. They are also available without backing for use when adding to existing insulation, as well as for places where a vapor barrier already exists.

The vapor-barrier side should always *face* the heated area, that is, the inside of a house. Note that a vapor barrier is effective only if it is

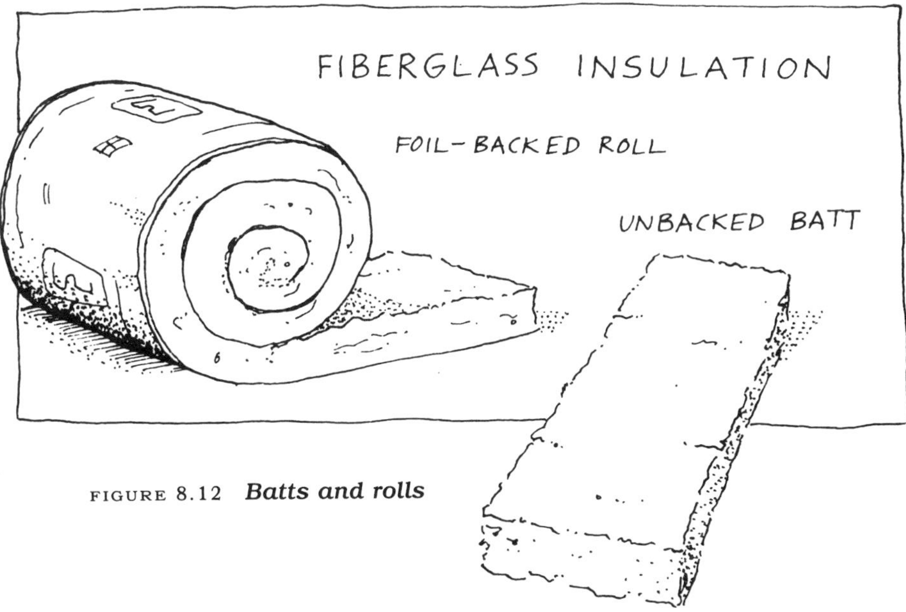

FIGURE 8.12 *Batts and rolls*

complete, that is, without breaks or openings of any kind. If you use backed insulation, therefore, you cannot leave any spaces between adjoining strips. If there is any question, it is advisable to cover the whole area with plastic sheeting (see chapter 9). Note that foil-backed insulation has a plus: the shiny aluminum has some value as a heat-reflecting surface.

FIGURE 8.13 *Orientation of backed insulation*

Rigid Insulation

Another type of insulation, which can sometimes be used in places such as the underside of floors, is sheet insulation made of hardened foam or polystyrene. It is easily cut to shape and, thickness for thickness, has a better R-factor than most other forms of insulation. On the other hand, it can also be flammable; because of that, many local building codes require gypsum wallboard to be used along with it. As a result, the job of installing it becomes heavier, more awkward, and more costly, seriously reducing its advantages.

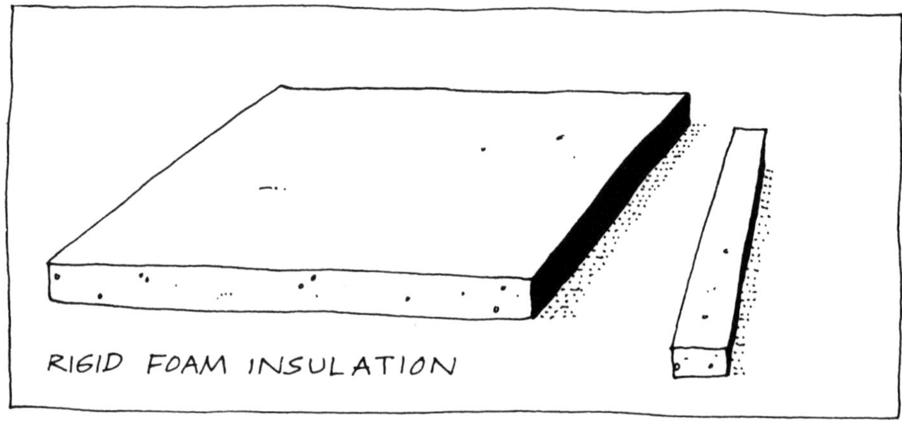

FIGURE 8.14 *Rigid foam insulation*

Blown-In Insulation

Probably the hardest place to insulate is in an already finished wall. In this situation your only recourse is blown-in insulation. Small holes, later plugged up and painted over, are drilled into the side of the house between every pair of studs or framing members. Insulation is then blown in under pressure through a hose.

There are two kinds of blown-in insulation: foam, which expands to fill every crevice and then dries, and loose cellulose or mineral wool, which, although considerably cheaper, may tend to settle over the years, leaving uninsulated gaps. Another disadvantage of the latter type is that small rodents love it, and they often tunnel through it and even carry some of it away to make nests.

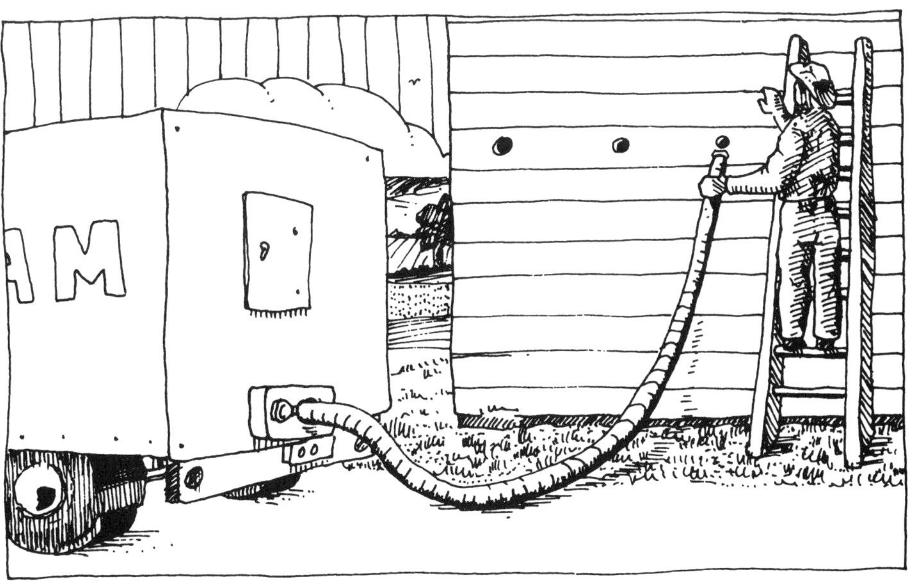

FIGURE 8.15 *Blown-in insulation*

Pipe Insulation

Since parts of the plumbing system may be exposed to freezing temperatures, they should either be wrapped in pipe insulation or protected with suitable lengths of electric heat tape. Plug these in when winter comes.

It also makes sense, at any time of the year, to insulate the hot-water pipes. That will prevent loss of heat before the water gets where it's going—and can cut down on your heating bill. For the same reason, hot-water heaters and storage tanks should also be insulated with wraps designed especially for that purpose.

NINE

Heating

Depending on the length and severity of the winter in your area, your heating system can be anything from large and complicated to simple and straightforward. Even in southern Florida and California, there is hardly a house that does not have some form of heating. No matter where you live, an annual inspection of what keeps you warm is in order. The best time to do this is early fall, before you need heating on a serious basis. Of course, even the most assiduous inspection cannot ensure uninterrupted operation, especially since you almost certainly depend partly on an outside energy source. But a well-maintained and conscientiously inspected system will certainly be the most efficient and economical to run.

GENERAL MAINTENANCE OF HEATING SYSTEMS

Most heating systems should be inspected by a qualified professional on an annual basis, right before the start of the heating season. Nevertheless, there is still a lot you can—and should—do yourself to make sure that every part of the system remains as trouble-free as possible.

Thermostats

Almost every form of automatic or semiautomatic heating is controlled by one or more thermostats. These precision instruments usually give years of trouble-free service. They require no servicing, no oiling, and, provided they are set correctly to begin with, no maintenance except an annual cleaning. Cleaning is important since the buildup of dust or other grime can keep them from operating properly.

There are two basic types of thermostats. The first depends on a little glass tube of mercury; the second, on a bimetallic strip.

Start by removing the face plate or front cover. If you see a small mercury-filled tube, use a small carpenter's level to make sure it is absolutely level. It may have been knocked or jarred and require readjustment. If it does, loosen the one or two screws holding the unit in place and move the whole thermostat until the tube itself is once again level.

If no mercury tube is visible, you probably have the bimetallic type, which is more easily affected by dirt. Unless the contact points are perfectly clean, the thermostat cannot function as a switch. You can see the points move as you adjust the temperature setting. Clean them as follows: Turn the thermostat to its lowest setting. The contact points should open enough for you to slip a thin piece of stiff paper (such as a business card) between them. Now turn the thermostat all the way up, causing the points to close on the card. Gently moving the card back and forth will clean the dirty points. Do not use sandpaper or emery cloth since these are too abrasive and will scratch the points, interfering with proper contact.

Alternatively, clean the points and other visible parts by brushing gently with a soft brush.

Electrical Baseboards

An electric heating system does not require much maintenance. Check the thermostats, as described above, and clean the heating units themselves. Usually a simple vacuuming is all that is necessary. If anything does go wrong, call an electrician; this is not a job for the do-it-yourselfer.

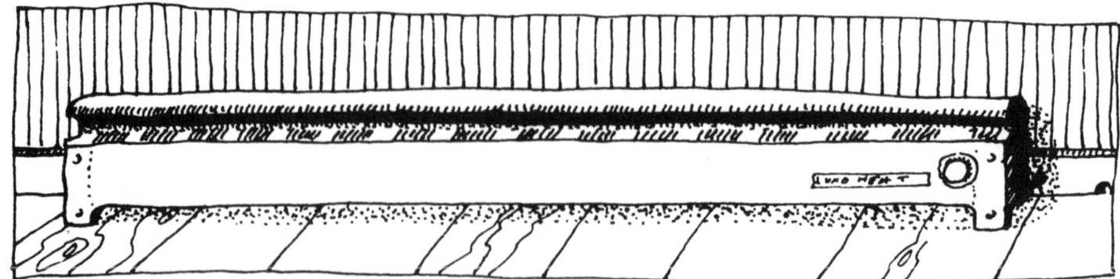

FIGURE 9.1 *Electrical baseboard unit*

Gas Heaters

Most gas utility companies will turn on, inspect, and adjust gas-fired heating systems as part of their service. If you operate a gas heater fueled by gas not provided by a municipal utility company—the gas is supplied from tanks at the house rather than through a municipal distribution system entering the house via a meter—you may have to assume more responsibility for the efficient operation of your system. Apart from adjusting the pilot-light levels and igniter controls, which the gas-supply company should do, the main job is keeping the unit clean. This means periodically removing grilles and covers and vacuuming out all dirt, dust, lint, and balls of fluff. Use a soft brush when cleaning around the controls.

Furnace Systems

A furnace, whether it's coal-, gas-, or oil-fired, and whether it runs a hot-air or a hot-water system, should be thoroughly overhauled before every heating season. Nearly all fuel companies offer a service contract that includes an annual cleaning and inspection, along with regular fuel delivery, plus a guarantee of immediate service should anything break down. Such a contract is by far the best way to take care of your heating system.

However, there remain a couple of things you should still attend to yourself. For hot-air systems, it is very important to replace the air filter (or filters) whenever it becomes dirty. How frequently this needs to be done depends on the particular situation of the furnace and how much dust and dirt are in the air. Start by checking the filter on a monthly basis, while the furnace is in use. Remove the filter from its

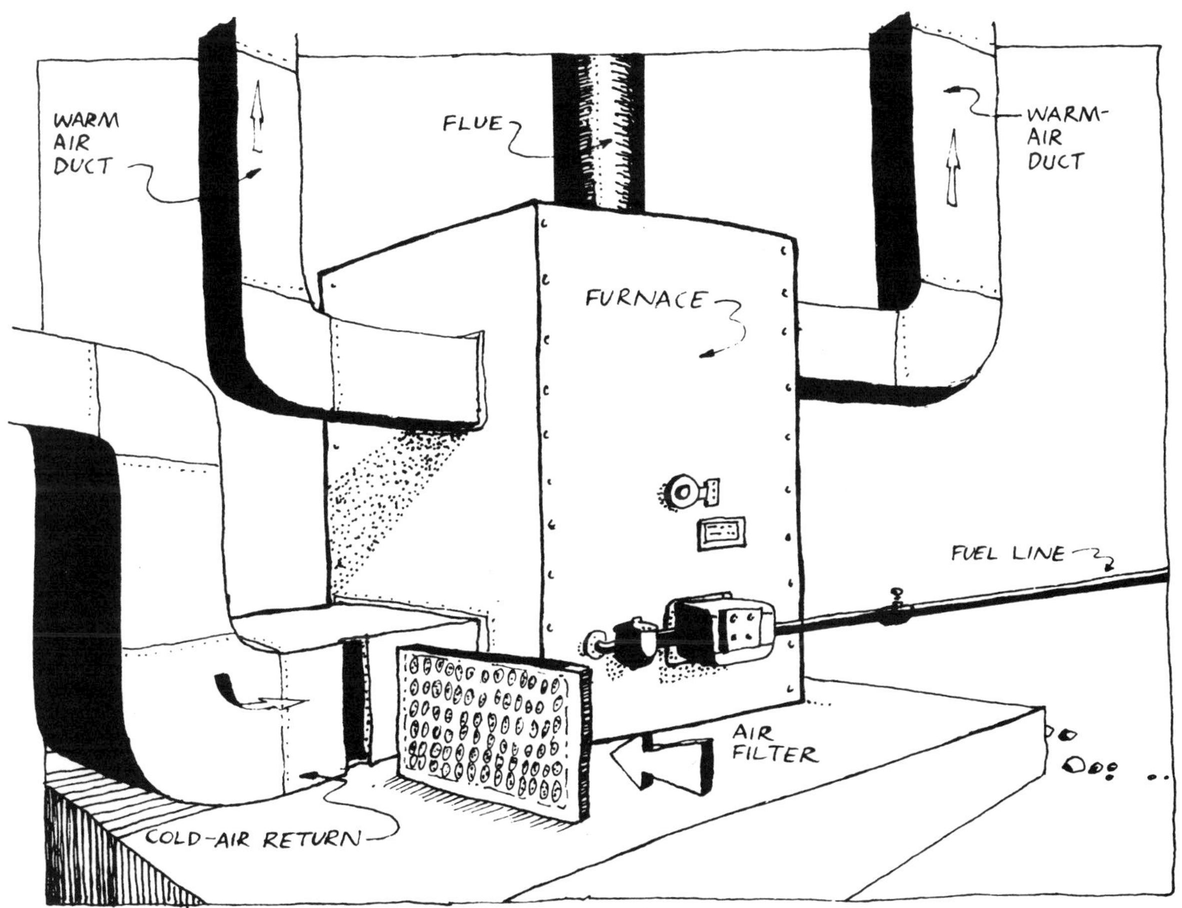

FIGURE 9.2 *Typical furnace*

slot in the cold-air return and hold it up to the light—you should still be able to see light through it. If not, replace it with a filter of the same size. You'll soon come to know how often you have to do this inspection. The simple operation of changing the air filter regularly can greatly improve the efficiency of the system, saving you money in the process.

Your other job is to see that all heat registers and grilles—whether floor-, wall-, or ceiling-mounted—are kept scrupulously clean and unobstructed. If you decide that a large piece of furniture, such as a cabinet or a couch, looks best right in front of a register, it may be worthwhile to have the register relocated. At least, keep such a register closed. Similarly, all other heating fixtures, such as baseboards, whether hot-water or electric, and radiators and convectors should be kept clean and unobstructed.

Fuel Tanks

Having overhauled the heating plant, it is now time to inspect the storage tanks. If you have an oil tank or an LP gas tank (for heating or cooking), it is a good idea to check it out before it is constantly being filled up and used in earnest.

Make sure that all tanks sit securely on a firm base. If they are located in the basement, a firm footing is probably not a problem, but many tanks are located outside, against or near the house. If winter frost or spring mud has caused the tanks to tilt or wobble, now is the time to rectify the situation.

While you're at it, check the fuel lines. They should be protected from rupturing as a result of the tank moving; they should also be insulated against freezing. This can be done by burying the lines, by wrapping them with insulation covered by waterproof tape, or, as a temporary measure, by packing the area under the tank (if that's where the fuel line emerges) with dead leaves or straw. (It is usually better to have the fuel line come out at the top of the tank to avoid its becoming clogged with sludge or sediment that might accumulate in the bottom of the tank.)

Oil tanks themselves can eventually rust out, often from the inside. Such rusting can cause actual leaks as well as blockages in the fuel

FIGURE 9.3 *Well-sited tank (being filled)*

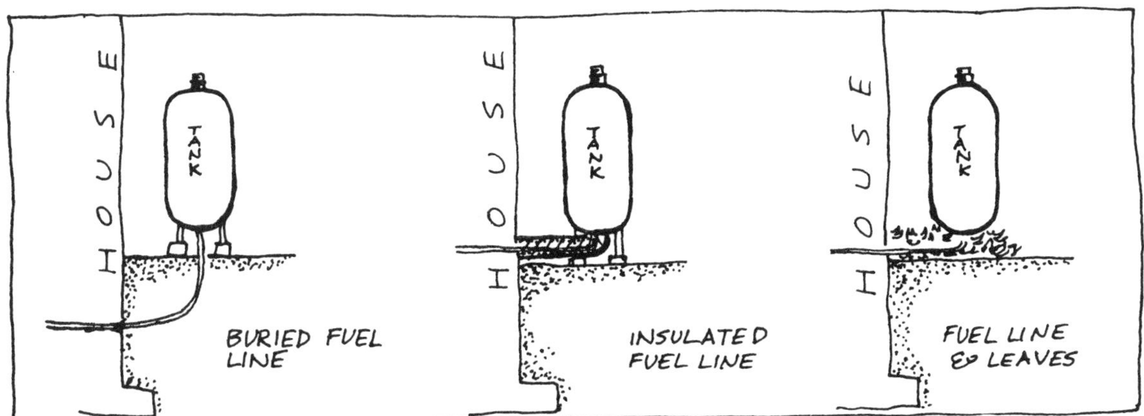

FIGURE 9.4 *Insulated fuel lines*

line. Internal rusting can be held at bay by the use of an anticondensation agent every time the tank is filled. Some oil companies will do this for you; some include such an agent in their oil. To minimize condensation, oil companies often recommend that you keep your tanks full during the whole year. External rusting is more easily controlled. Simply scrape it away as soon as it appears, and paint the tank with a rustproofing metal paint. These paints are available in various colors, and a well-painted tank looks better against the side of the house than a grimy, oil-stained, rusty one.

It is also good insurance to add a cleaning and anticondensation ingredient to the oil storage tank every time the tank is refilled. Available at most hardware stores, this product comes in liquid form, with label information on the correct quantity to add.

FIGURE 9.5 *Tank maintenance*

Chimneys and Fireplaces

Chimneys are potentially the most dangerous part of any combusting heating system. Although there is little that is cheerier than a brightly burning fire in the fireplace, chimneys of wood stoves and fireplaces especially are vulnerable to disaster if ignored season after season. Aside from the problem of deteriorating masonry (see chapter 2), buildups of soot and creosote may cause a chimney fire, which can endanger the whole house. To ward off the latter problem, it is important to keep the chimney clean.

It is difficult to give a rule for how often a chimney needs cleaning. It depends on the kind of fuel being combusted and, in the case of wood, the species being burned—softwoods and unseasoned material produce more creosote than well-seasoned material and most hardwoods. Other considerations are how frequently the chimney is used and how hot the burning temperatures are—a hotter fire leaves less residue since material is more fully consumed. The construction and location of the chimney itself are also important variables. At the very least, an inspection should be performed once a season, preferably twice. If an inspection demonstrates a serious need for cleaning, perform the next inspection after a shorter interval. Apart from a possible decrease in the drawing ability of the chimney (a draught test should be part of a furnace servicing), the first indication that you may have of a serious buildup could well be a chimney fire; hence the need for preventive maintenance.

The typical chimney can be most easily cleaned by stuffing a sack

FIGURE 9.6 *Cheery fireplace*

with crumpled-up newspapers and a few rocks added for weight, and lowering it down the chimney on the end of a long rope. Doing this operation a few times should dislodge most of the soot and creosote in the flue, so take the proper precautions at the bottom end before you begin.

After cleaning, a masonry chimney should be inspected for cracks or crumbling; the flashing around the roof and chimney should be checked for holes or corrosion; the spark arrester (if there is one, it is usually a mesh cap that fits over the top of the chimney) should be examined to make sure that it is in good condition; and the cleanout door (generally located at the base of the chimney on the outside) should be checked to ensure that it closes tightly, after having cleaned out any accumulated soot, of course. One last check is to confirm that the damper is working and not stuck in one position, rusted out, or otherwise deteriorated.

Metal chimneys, usually encased in a spacious wooden framework, are becoming increasingly common. Not only are they much quicker and cheaper to build, now that technology has made possible the fabrication of well-insulated, long-lasting units, but they are not subject to much of the deterioration that can beset a masonry chimney—not the least of which can be the devastating effects of an earthquake. Metal flues may be cleaned the same way as masonry chimneys, and the same attention should be given to the chimney casing where it abuts the house, as well as to the cap and spark arrester.

Freestanding metal chimneys—of the type commonly used in wood stoves that are not installed in preexisting fireplaces—often consist of a single thickness of metal. This kind can ultimately rust away owing to the deleterious effect of combined heat and cold on a single layer of metal. For this reason, newer metal chimneys are all double-

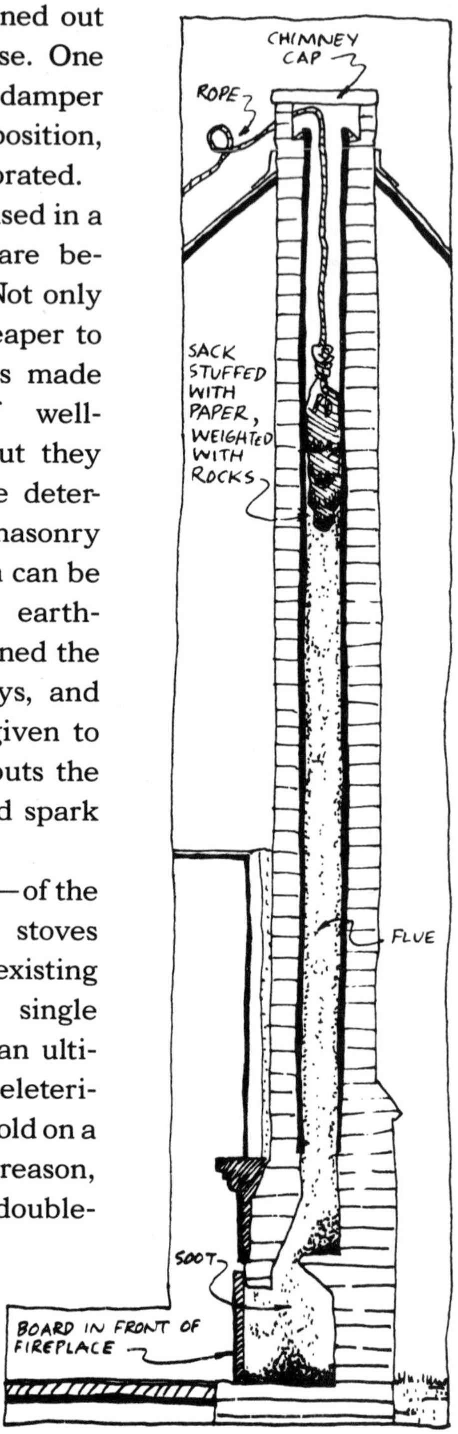

FIGURE 9.7 *Chimney cleaning*

skinned. Both single- and double-skinned chimneys should be thoroughly cleaned. Especially important with stovepipes is to ensure that there is adequate insulation at the point where the pipe passes through the roof or the wall (see chapter 8).

Storing Wood

If you heat with wood, or simply use your fireplace a lot, experience will soon teach you how and where best to store your wood. The woodpile must be conveniently located near the house and at least somewhat protected. It should be stacked so as to allow ventilation through the wood. With ventilation, the wood will age better, stay dryer, and be less likely to rot.

If you keep logs in the house, clean out their storage area often, for you may be bringing unwanted insects into the house along with the firewood.

HUMIDITY

Once the heating system has been working for a while, the moisture content of the house will have reached its winter level. Too much or too little moisture in the air can have harmful effects on you, your house, and the items in it—especially wood furniture.

Very simply, adequate moisture in the air cuts heating costs and increases comfort by making the temperature in the house more uniform. Insufficient moisture or humidity can dry out you and your furniture (causing the latter to shrink and crack). On the other hand, excessive humidity can lead to condensation problems such as rotted woodwork and stained ceilings and walls.

To avoid damage to expensive wood furniture and high-quality pianos and other delicate wooden instruments, it is often necessary to take extensive precautions to control the humidity in the house. Even an ordinary piano will exhibit dramatic changes in pitch when subjected to changes in humidity; unless you keep a sharp eye on and heed the warnings of the *hygrometer*—an inexpensive instrument for measuring humidity—the piano tuner will be an all-too-frequent visitor.

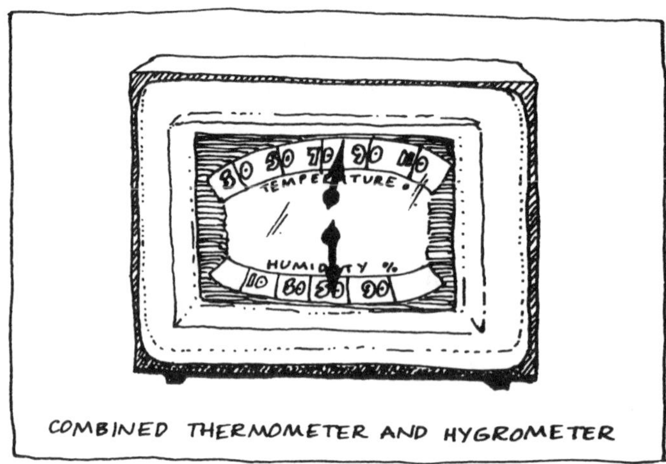

FIGURE 9.8 *Combined thermometer and hygrometer*

The hygrometer shows the percentage of moisture in the surrounding air. Frequently included with thermometers, hygrometers are designed to hang on a wall or sit on a shelf. If cracks appear in unfinished (or even finished) wood surfaces, if the gap between cupboard or cabinet doors and their frames seems to be widening, if you wake up parched and thirsty every morning, then the hygrometer's needle will probably be pointing to a very low number. On the other hand, if every time the temperature drops outside (a) your windows drip with water on the inside, (b) your supply of postage stamps is all stuck together, and (c) every door in the house becomes hard to open, then you will doubtlessly observe a very high reading on the hygrometer.

How much the humidity changes depends a lot on the kind of heating system you have in your house. A wood stove will dry out any moisture in the air very quickly. For this reason, many people keep large kettles of water simmering on top of their wood stove—the steam that escapes helps replace the evaporated moisture in the air.

Similarly, hot-air heating systems can be very drying, although if the cold-air return part of the system is located in a damp basement, some dampness will be pumped into the house as moisture in the hot air. This is not often the case, however, since the cold-air return is usually located *within* the house. In this situation the only solution is to install a humidifier in the hot-air system, which will help keep the

FIGURE 9.9 *Replacing lost moisture*

hot air at the desired level of humidity. (Figure 9.10 illustrates these two situations: In *a,* the hot-air system draws in damp air from the basement and pumps moist hot air into the house. In *b,* the hot-air system gets its cold air from within the house, then heats it and pumps it back in; the basement, even if it is damp, remains separated from the house [and the cold-air return] by a vapor barrier.)

Electric heat is less drying than hot-air heat, but the most comfortable of all—insofar as humidity is concerned—is a hot-water system, using either radiators or baseboard units. However, since you're probably not going to change your heating system because of a humidity problem, the only thing to do is to install a humidifier to replace the lost moisture.

On the other hand, if your problem is too much humidity, you can always install a dehumidifier—usually in the basement, since this is likely to be the source of the excess moisture. (See Ratings of dehumidifiers in the appendix.) If your heating system does not draw air from the basement (because it is a closed system using electricity or hot water), installing a vapor barrier between the basement and the house (as shown at *b* in figure 9.10) will help considerably.

Every house should have vapor barriers surrounding the living space to prevent condensation from forming in the outside walls and the roof. Even a house with a comfortable and correct humidity level

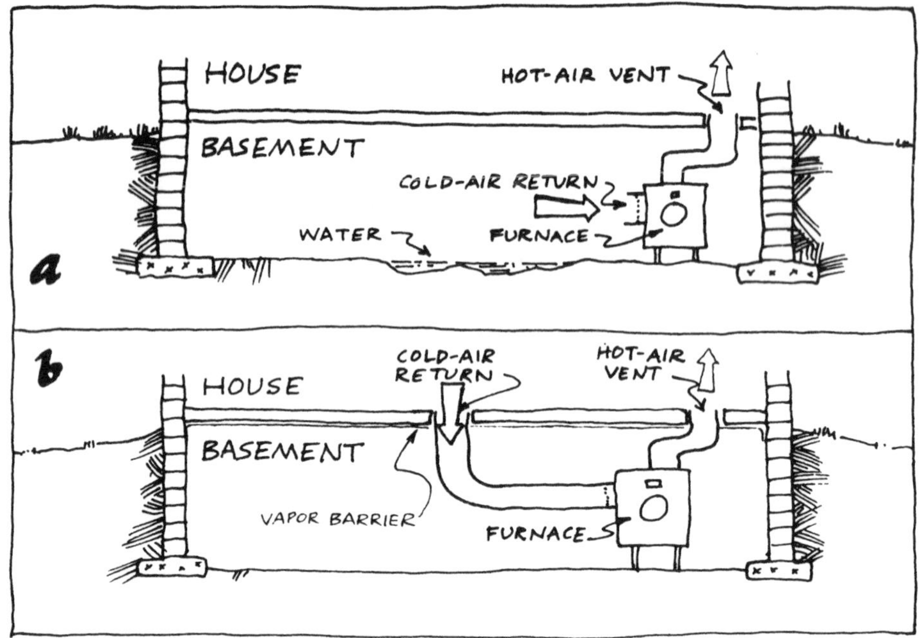

FIGURE 9.10 *Effect of location of cold-air return*

can have sufficient moisture in the air to cause condensation if this air comes into contact with cold exterior walls. Theoretically, the house should be insulated well enough so that the warm air inside cannot reach the inside surfaces of the exterior walls of the house, but this is rarely possible. The only way to prevent such condensation is some form of vapor barrier on the room side of the insulation.

Some types of insulation are sold with a paper or foil backing that is supposed to reflect heat back into the house and act as a vapor barrier. It may do the former, but it cannot do the latter unless it is absolutely continuous over the wall or ceiling surface involved. Even the slightest gap or unsealed joint between rolls (of insulation), not to mention tears in the backing, will allow moist air through. The only truly effective barrier is a skin of plastic covering the entire room. The plastic should be installed after the insulation has been put in place, and the sheets should overlap well and be taped tightly at the joints.

Windows, of course, represent a gap in the vapor barrier and can

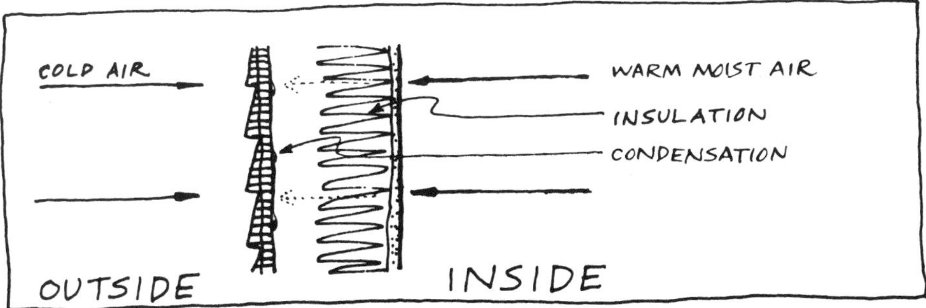

FIGURE 9.11 *Formation of condensation*

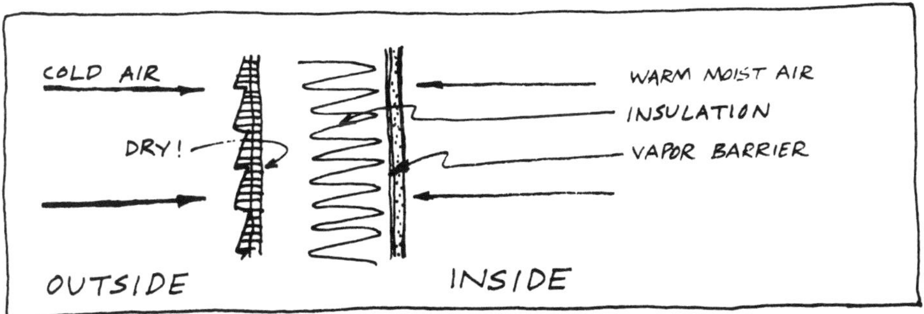

FIGURE 9.12 *Prevention of condensation*

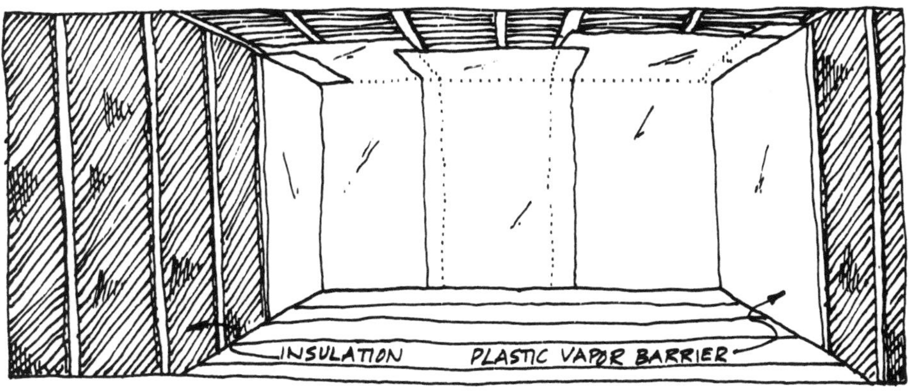

FIGURE 9.13 *Interior vapor barrier*

be the first places where you see condensation. The warm moist inside air hits the cold glass; the moisture condenses into water droplets and runs down the inside of the window. As it becomes even colder outside, this condensed moisture can freeze, and you can wake up to a Jack Frost effect on the inside of your windows. Then, as the heat comes up, the ice melts, causing a pool on the sill. Eventually, the paint job on the windows and woodwork deteriorates.

The cure in this case is to install storm windows or double-glazing (see chapter 8). As a temporary measure, you can tack a sheet of

FIGURE 9.14 *Condensed moisture on windows*

plastic over the entire window, on the inside or the outside (it's less vulnerable on the inside). The principle behind two layers of glass (or a layer of glass and a layer of plastic) is that the sandwich of air prevents the cold from the outside reaching the inside glass; at the same time, the moist interior air cannot reach the cold outer glass. This not only solves your condensation problem but provides excellent insulation.

Installing a vapor barrier after a house is finished is an almost impossible job, since it involves removing all the finished interior surfaces, whether gypsum wallboard, plaster, or paneling. In such a case, the only practical solution to excessive humidity is a dehumidifier. Controlling the humidity and keeping all the moisture in the air inside the house is the best thing you can do for your exterior walls and roof. Over the years, condensation in the outer walls will cause rot and decay as well as peeling paint on the outside of the house.

INSECT PROBLEMS IN WINTER

If you should lose heat for a period—because of a power outage—you can take minor advantage of the situation in at least one way. By midwinter, most insects are either dead, with only eggs surviving to perpetuate the species in the spring, or asleep somewhere oblivious to snow and cold. However, given the right environment, such as a nice warm attic, many can do quite well. On a bright sunny day you can often see semistuporous flies walking about the windowpanes. Fleas, similarly protected by a warm domestic environment, can also survive, their numbers undiminished, on rugs and dogs. Should you discover a plague of insects at this time of year—and were the heating system to shut down—you can eliminate the insects by simply freezing them out. Open the doors and windows and let the cold in for a short while—not long enough to freeze any pipes or do any damage, but long enough to destroy the pests.

T E N

The Tool Kit and Emergency Supplies

Many repairs—and all emergencies—know no season. Once you take up residence in a house, prudence and common sense dictate certain obligations and responsibilities on your part. Fulfilling them not only ensures the efficient functioning of the house—making it as comfortable and as convenient for you as possible—but also means that emergencies can be dealt with safely and with a minimum of disruption.

A HOUSEHOLD TOOL KIT

Although you may not actually perform the maintenance or repairs described in this book, every houseowner should possess a few basic tools.

It should be said at the outset that cheap, poor-quality tools are worse than useless. A hammer that breaks or bends the first time you use it or a screwdriver that twists like a pretzel or continually slips out of the screw slot is not worth even the small amount it may have cost. Not only will such tools not do their job, thereby frustrating or discouraging you, but they may actually be unsafe. So if you have only one hammer, make it a good one. If you know nothing about

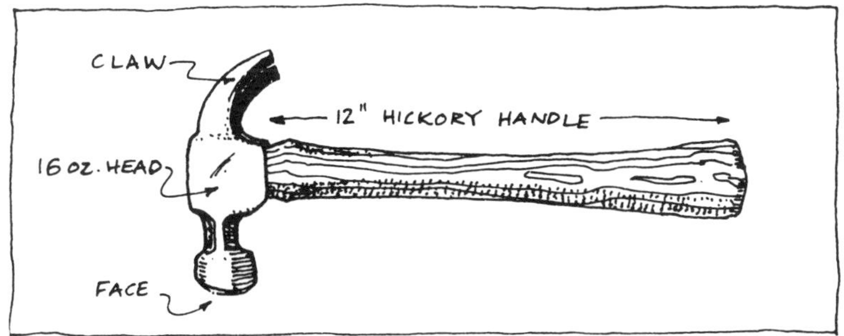

FIGURE 10.1 *A good hammer*

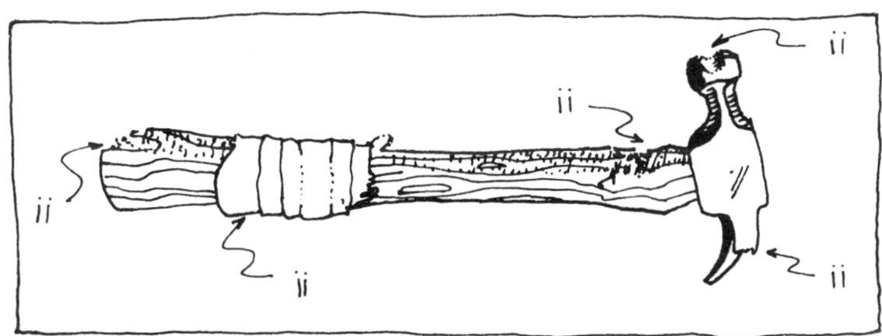

FIGURE 10.2 *An abused hammer*

tools, ask for "the best" at the hardware store. If you buy the best, it will last for a long time, probably as long as you live in your house.

The next point to be made about tools is that although they are designed to do a lot of work—and some of it very hard work—few tools remain useful if they are abused or not attended to once in a while. Abuse may be of two kinds: passive and active. Passive abuse results from throwing your tools together higgledy-piggledy so they bang against one another, dulling edges that ought to be sharp, or scratching, denting, and even bending parts so that they don't function properly. If the pile of tools is in a damp corner, so much the worse—they'll start to rust. Active abuse results from using the wrong tool for the job—using a chisel as a screwdriver, or a hammer as a prybar, for example—as well as using the tool foolishly or incorrectly.

Aside from a hammer and a couple of screwdrivers (a straight

FIGURE 10.3 *The right screwdriver for the right screw*

screwdriver and a Phillips-head screwdriver for cross-slotted screws—see figure 10.3), equip the house with a pair of pliers, an adjustable wrench, and an electric drill with a set of drill bits.

With these few tools you can make almost any emergency repair, at least temporarily. You'll also find them useful dozens of times for small jobs, such as hanging pictures, making wire connections, and tightening loose nuts on appliances. If you add a saw—almost any kind, from a hacksaw to a handsaw—and a metal tape measure, you'll have the beginnings of a real tool kit. You may even start thinking about a few projects that go beyond simple repairs.

These basic tools are the absolute minimum you should have. Even if you don't plan to do anything around the house yourself, owning these tools will enable a willing friend to help you in an emergency—and perhaps save you from incurring hefty bills from professionals.

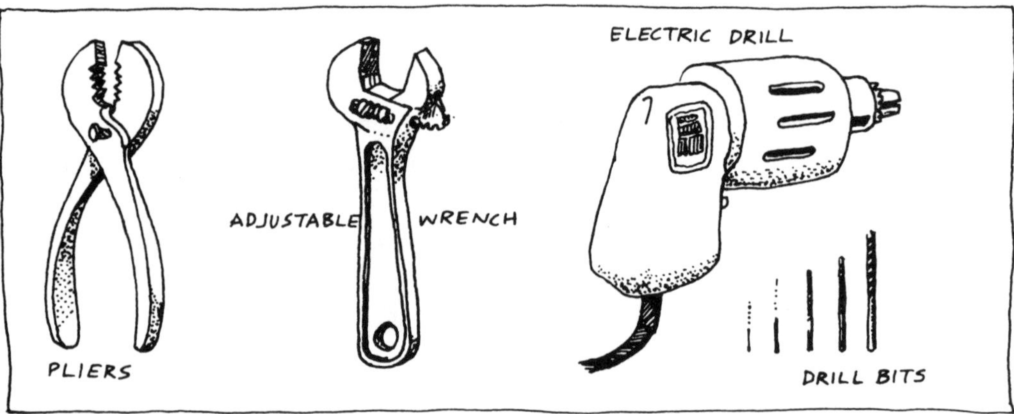

FIGURE 10.4 ***Pliers, adjustable wrench, and drill***

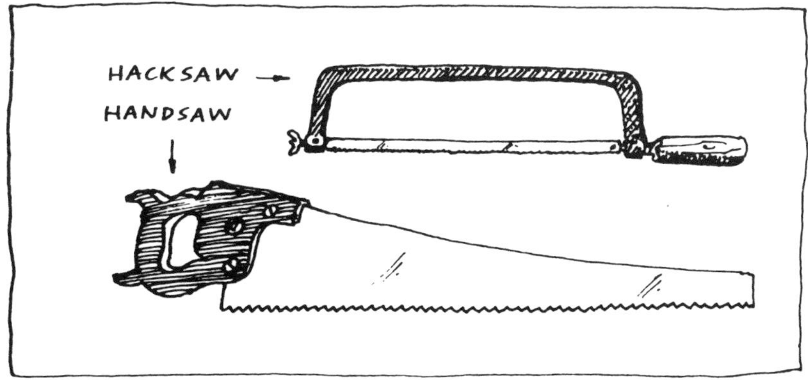

FIGURE 10.5 *Saws*

If you're interested enough to go beyond this list, you may well enjoy tools for their own sake and may also develop an interest in carpentry and fixing things. You'll discover, or have discovered already, that there is an almost infinite number of tools designed for every conceivable application. (See Ratings for cordless screwdrivers and sanders in the appendix.)

Whether you limit yourself to just these tools or not, try to hang as many of them up as possible rather than throwing them all together in a box. A well-organized toolbox may be the hallmark of a fine artisan, but a small collection of household tools often tends to get lost and damaged in a box stuffed under the sink or at the back of a linen closet. The one tool you want is invariably buried under all the others, and if tools are hard to reach, the jobs may be postponed or disregarded.

Check that all the tools are present and hung up where they should be. Squirt a drop of oil on joints and moving parts. Make sure there is no rust anywhere; if there is, rub it off with fine steel wool or emery paper. Determine whether the hammerhead is loose; if it is—and if it has a wooden handle—get an extra wedge from the hardware store and drive it in the eye of the head (where the end of the handle is visible). And last, if the edge of your straight screwdriver has rounded over, file it square again.

Stepladder

Regardless of the household chore, a safe and secure stepladder is a necessary adjunct to any tool collection. To make sure you choose the right one, look for the following characteristics:

- *Resistance to sway.* Sway means the side-to-side movement that ladders make when you are standing on the highest safe step. As a class, aluminum and fiberglass-aluminum ladders prove to be more rigid than wood models.
- *Resistance to "walking."* A ladder should keep its feet firmly on the floor even as you shift your weight from side to side. Every ladder can walk, but some ladders do it more readily than others.
- *Resistance to tipping.* A stepladder should stay put when you try to climb up while carrying a bulky load in one hand. Ladders with a wide front-to-back stance are less tippy than ones with fairly steep sides.

A well-made ladder also has hinges and pivots that move smoothly and easily, so you can set up the ladder or fold it in one smooth operation. Check ladders in the store first to see how smoothly they operate.

A six-foot ladder generally represents a more practical choice than an eight-footer because it's easier to carry and jockey around. You can safely stand about four feet off the ground on a six-foot ladder; that's high enough for even a short person to reach an eight-foot ceiling. (See Ratings on stepladders in the appendix.)

EMERGENCY SUPPLIES

Despite the best preparations and precautions, emergencies can and do occur, through no fault of our own. Most of us are to a greater or lesser extent dependent on a complicated "life-support" system over which we have no real control. Nearly all of our houses are hooked into municipal utilities; we are dependent on automobiles; and we rely on a variety of regular services that enable us to function "normally." When one part of this system breaks down, the consequences can be uncomfortable and, on rare occasions, dangerous. By taking the following measures, you can minimize discomfort and property damage during an emergency.

Because it is so easy to take things for granted, make it a point once a year to check on emergency supplies. For people who live in cold areas, for example, a backup heating system is very important, not only because of discomfort, but to avoid the potential danger of frozen pipes, leaks, and serious damage to the house. If you normally use a central heating system but have a fireplace or wood stove, keep a supply of firewood on hand in case of a breakdown or power outage. (Kerosene heaters are *not* recommended because of the danger of fire and the problem of fumes in an indoor environment.)

Emergency light is the next most important item to be considered. Put a couple of flashlights (with extra batteries) in different places in your house. Candles are easy to keep, but check once in a while that your supply is adequate for a long night. They should be kept where they can be found easily in a hurry—and in the dark. If you are subject to more than the rare power outage in your area, consider a backup generator. At the very least, have some major battery-operated lamps at the ready.

A battery-powered radio, with extra batteries, is another important item in your emergency arsenal. A supply of bulbs and fuses is also a good thing to keep on hand.

Last, but certainly not least, every conscientious homeowner should maintain a basic first-aid kit, and, almost as important, a readily available list of emergency phone numbers. This list should include not only those for doctors and hospitals but also numbers for the police, the fire department, a plumber available 24 hours a day, electricians, and other professional help.

You can, of course, go on to prepare for any conceivable disaster by installing an extra water tank, a fallout shelter, and stores of dry food.

If you live in an area prone to natural disasters—earthquakes, floods, forest fires, tornadoes, or hurricanes—you should be aware of the special circumstances surrounding them and take additional precautions. In areas where hurricanes are frequent, it's a good idea to keep a supply of plywood with which windows and other large areas of glass can be protected against high winds. The best defense against tornadoes is to retreat below ground level—to a secure basement, for example, provided with its own lighting, even if this is no more than a flashlight or two.

Residents in earthquake country are continually encouraged to keep on hand at least a couple of days' supply of water and food, as well as emergency heating and lighting and a good supply of batteries for portable radios. Local authorities are responsible for the security of municipal utilities, but the individual homeowner must know how to turn off the gas supply and the water mains, must make sure that the water heater is firmly strapped to the wall, and must protect against objects falling in a big quake (securing tall pieces of furniture, providing cabinets with secure catches, and so forth).

Appendix
Master Checklist

The following list includes the most important items that should be checked at least once a year. Each item is referenced to the chapter or chapters in which it is discussed, so you can easily find a more detailed discussion of what's involved. If you can make the necessary check at least once in any 12-month period, you can rest assured that you have done everything that ought to be done.

AIR VENTS: for clean air flow 2, 5, 6, 8
ATTIC INSULATION: for completeness 5
ATTIC LOUVERS: for condition of screens 5, 6
BASEMENT: for masonry decay, wood rot, insect damage, and flooding or standing water 1, 2, 5
BASEMENT VENTS: opening and closing 2, 8
BRICKWORK: for efflorescence and spalling 2
CAULKING: of joints and cracks 2, 4, 8
CHIMNEY: for cracks, dirt, spark arresters, and flashing 2, 9
CONCRETE: for cracks and chips 2
CULVERTS AND DITCHES: for leaves and debris, free flow, and sufficiency 1, 7
CUPBOARDS AND ATTICS: for pest infestations 2, 5
DRIVEWAY: for cracks, puddles, potholes, and snowplow markers 1, 7

SUMP PUMP: for efficient operation	2, 3
TOOLS, HOUSEHOLD AND GARDEN: for repair or replacement	1, 2, 7, 10
VENT STACK: for blockages	3
WALLS AND FENCES: for condition and placement	1, 7
WEATHERSTRIPPING: on doors and windows	8
WELL: for quality and quantity of water supply	3
WINDOWS: for glass and putty, paint and rot	2, 4
WOOD SIDING: for paint condition and rot	2, 4

Product Ratings

Dehumidifiers

Like an air conditioner, a dehumidifier wrings the moisture out of indoor air on a sultry day. There, the resemblance ends. An air conditioner pumps the heat and moisture outdoors. But once a dehumidifier has condensed moisture out of the air, it passes the air across a set of warm coils and back into the room. The air is drier—but also warmer than before.

Even though a dehumidifier probably won't make you more comfortable in the summer, it can dry out the chronically damp air that makes water pipes sweat, tools rust, and that gives a room that musty smell.

Size—that is, the amount of moisture the dehumidifier can remove in a day—matters most. The larger a dehumidifier's rated capacity, the better. Units that claim to remove 40 to 50 pints per day tend to do their job faster and more efficiently than smaller models. And whereas a large dehumidifier can always be throttled back, a small one can't always be turned up enough to bring humidity down to a tolerable level.

Ratings of Dehumidifiers

◉ ◓ ○ ◒ ●

Better ◀——▶ *Worse*

Listed in order of estimated quality. Essentially similar models are bracketed and listed alphabetically.

❶ Price. Manufacturer's suggested retail; + indicates shipping is extra; * indicates price paid (manufacturer did not provide suggested price). Except for mail-order brands, discounts are generally available.

❷ Capacity. As stated by the manufacturer, based on a standard test to measure how many pints of water the unit can remove from the air in a day. The rated capacity can help you narrow the choice of models (bigger is better), but it may not be a meaningful guide to performance in extreme conditions.

❸ Moisture removal. As measured by Consumers Union, with each model running continuously at its highest fan speed. The scores in these five columns are based on the amount of water actually removed, without regard to the unit's rated capacity. The **80°/60% humidity** score corresponds to the industry's standard test. Only the *Friedrich/Penney/White-Westinghouse* triplets and the *Oasis* were 10 percent below their rated capacity, on average. The **70°/70%** score reflects performance in the typical damp basement. The **90°/50%** score covers the kind of extreme conditions you might encounter in the height of summer; differences in scores between this test and the 80°/60% test reflect a drop of 4 to 5 pints per day in water extraction. The **low temperature** test was particularly stressful, because ice can form on the coils below about 65°, and dehumidification stops. The best units in this test managed to extract only about 30 pints of water a day. Finally, the **brownout** test reflects performance at reduced voltage in a 90° room. The best could run satisfactorily even at 100 volts.

❹ Energy efficiency. The best extracted about 2½ pints of water for every kilowatt-hour of energy consumed; the worst extracted about 2 pints per kwh.

As published in a July 1990 issue of Consumer Reports.

Brand and model	Price ❶	Capacity, pt. ❷	❸ *Moisture removal*: 80°/60%	70°/70%	90°/50%	Low temperature	Brownout	Energy efficiency ❹	Advantages	Disadvantages	Comments
Sears Cat. No. 5548	$292+	48	◉	◓	○	◓	◉	◓	C,G,H	—	C
Emerson Quiet Kool DG50F	320	50	◉	◉	◓	◉	◓	◓	D,E,I,K	a	E
Friedrich FD50X	360	50	◓	◉	○	①	◓	○	A,B,C	c,d	A
J.C. Penney Cat. No. 857-0137	300+	50	◓	◉	○	①	◓	○	A,B,C	c,d	A
White-Westinghouse ED508K	299	50	◓	◉	○	①	◓	○	A,B,C	c,d	A
Emerson Quiet Kool DG40F	280	40	○	○	◒	◓	◉	◉	D,E,I,K	a	E
Sears Cat. No. 5540	271+	40	○	○	◒	◉	◉	◉	C	—	C
Crosley DH40J7	278	40	○	◒	○	○	◉	◓	A,B,F	c,d	—
Oasis OD-50L	427*	55	◓	◓	○	●	◓	◓	B,D,J	d,e,f	B
Hunter 31040	280	40	◒	◒	◒	◉	◓	◓	D,E,L	b,d	D

① *Performance of these essentially similar models varied considerably in this test.*

Specifications and Features

All: • Weigh 50 to 60 lb. • Have adjustable humidistat. • Have removable water container, with signal light to show when container is full and automatic shutoff to prevent overflow. • Have current draw of 6 to 9 amp at 120 volts, which may increase under extreme conditions.

Except as noted, all: • Can dispose of water through a hose after you drill open a coupling molded into water container. • Are 20½ in. high, 12½ to 13½ in. wide, 17 to 19½ in. deep overall. • Have parts-and-labor warranty on entire unit for first year, on sealed refrigeration system for second to fifth year.

Key to Advantages

A—Partly enclosed water container with handle; easy to carry without spilling.
B--Water container easy to position properly inside unit.
C—Unit won't operate unless water container is properly installed; relatively unlikely to drip.
D—Has open connection for drain hose.
E—Open area in base allows water to flow directly into floor drain.
F—Controls conveniently mounted on top of unit, under transparent shield.
G—Separate switch lets unit be turned on or off without disturbing humidistat setting; fan can be set to run with compressor off.
H—Has two-speed fan; relatively quiet at low speed.
I— Has single fan speed, but still relatively quiet.
J— Water container easy to clean.
K—Has air filter.
L—Has humidity meter.

Key to Disadvantages

a— Flimsy float arm can be bent by accident; bent arm makes it hard to replace water container after emptying and can make it seem container is properly positioned when it actually bypasses automatic shutoff.
b— String on float lets you lift it out of the way when removing water container; not very convenient.
c— Water container somewhat difficult to clean.
d— Humidistat not as well marked as others.
e— Humidistat required rather critical adjustment to achieve desired conditions.
f— More difficult to maneuver than most; has only two wheels, not casters.

Key to Comments

A—Has two-speed fan; noisy on higher speed, but relatively quiet on low.
B—Smaller than most, 15¼ in. high and 14¼ in. deep.
C—Has fragrance dispenser.
D—Has extended warranty only on compressor, not on entire sealed refrigeration system.
E—Discontinued. **DG50F** replaced by essentially identical **DH50F, DG40F** replaced by essentially identical **DH40F.**

Stepladders

Let safety be your guide when buying a stepladder. You'll want a ladder that will be secure and stable underfoot. Some 29 stepladders were tested for this report, a selection that reflects the variety you'll find at hardware stores and home centers. Safety was the main concern.

Look to an aluminum ladder for ordinary chores in or around the house. Judging from the tests, aluminum ladders are generally steadier than wood ones, they weigh less, and they won't loosen up with use. But if you spend a lot of time working outside with electric tools or around the power lines that enter your house, then your safest bet is a wood or fiberglass/aluminum ladder. They won't conduct electricity as an aluminum stepladder will.

You can easily check the ladders in the store to see how smoothly they operate. At the same time, check the design of the spreaders, the hinged metal arms that hold the ladder open. Some have a single pivot in the middle, a design that can pinch your fingers. A better design has two pivot points; some ladders have pinchless sides: rails that stay a finger's width apart when the ladder is folded.

Ratings of Stepladders

Listed by type. Within types, listed by height in order of estimated quality, based primarily on safety and on convenience as judged by a panel of users.

❶ **Brand and model.** The fiberglass/aluminum models are popular with contractors. The others are sold primarily to do-it-yourselfers. Fiberglass/aluminum and wood ladders can safely be used anywhere. Aluminum ladders should not be used outdoors with electric tools because the ladders can conduct electricity. If you can't find a model, call the company.

❷ **Price.** The average price paid. A + indicates that shipping was extra.

❸ **Working load.** Manufacturers' claims for the maximum weight a ladder should bear, as determined in standard industry tests. These figures correspond to the weight limits in the duty rating displayed on each ladder. For safety's sake, your weight plus that of the materials you bring onto the ladder with you should never exceed the working load. A 200- or 225-pound working load is enough for most people.

❹ **Resistance to swaying.** A key judgment from panelists. It shows the stability of a ladder as you climb, shifting your weight from step to step, or perch on the highest step you can safely occupy.

❺ **Resistance to "walking."** This panel test judgment shows which ladders are most likely to chatter along the floor as you shift your weight from step to step. A ladder that "walks" too much can scuff the floor, upset a can of paint, or even make you fall.

❻ **Resistance to tipping.** Panelists gauged tippiness by putting one foot on the ladder's lowest step and grabbing the ladder with one hand while carrying a small but bulky load in the other. The wider the angle between an

As published in a September 1990 issue of Consumer Reports.

❶ *Brand and model*	❷ *Price*	*Weight*	❸ *Working load*	*Resistance to* ❹ *Swaying*	❺ *"Walking"*	❻ *Tipping*	*Ease of* ❼ *Opening & closing*	❽ *Carrying*	❾ *Moving*	*Advantages*	*Disadvantages*	*Comments*
Fiberglass/aluminum, 6-ft.												
Keller 976	$92	21 lb.	300 lb.	◉	○	○	◉	○	◓	A,B	—	*A,E*
Werner 7206	168	23	300	◉	○	◓	◓	○	○	A,E	h	*A,E*
Aluminum, 6-ft.												
Werner 376	120	14	250	◓	○	◒	◉	◓	◓	A,B,C,D,E,F	—	*A,C*
Keller 916	63	17	250	◓	◓	◒	◓	○	○	B,C,D	—	*A*
Keller Greenline 926	53	12	225	◓	○	◒	◓	◓	◓	B,C,D	—	*A*
Keller 936	48	11	200	◓	○	◒	○	◓	◓	B,C,D	—	*A*
Sears Craftsman 42386	58+	14	225	◓	◒	○	◓	◓	◓	A,D	c,h	*A,G,H*
White Metal Wonderlight 21006	67	11	225	◓	◒	◒	◒	◓	◓	D	c,h	*G*
Werner 366	74	12	225	○	◒	◒	◒	◓	◓	A,B,C,F	—	*A*
Sears Craftsman 42156	40	11	200	◓	◒	◒	○	◓	◓	D	f,h	*H*
White Metal Easylight 31106	42	10	200	◓	◒	◒	○	◓	◓	D	f,h	—
Werner 356	60	12	200	○	◒	◒	●	◓	◓	B,F	—	*A*
Aluminum, 8-ft.												
Keller Greenline 928	93	17	225	○	◒	◓	◉	○	◒	C,D	h	*A*
White Metal Heartsaver 22008	81	17	225	◓	◒	◒	○	○	◒	A,D	c,h	*A,G*
Sears Craftsman 42388	79	18	225	◓	◒	◒	◒	○	◒	A,D	h	*A,G,H*
Wood, 6-ft.												
Werner W356	29	20	200	○	○	◓	◉	○	○	A,B,D	d	—
Werner W366	58	22	225	○	○	○	◓	◓	◒	A,B,D,F	—	*A*
Putnam Peerless	59	22	225	◒	○	◓	◉	○	○	A,D	h	*D*
Sears 40116	20	17	200	◒	◒	◒	◉	○	◓	A,D	b	*B,H*
Lynn No. 76 Supertred SUS06	58	21	225	◒	○	◓	◓	○	○	A,B,D	a,g	—
Werner W336	38	17	200	◒	○	○	◓	◓	○	A,B,D,F	d,g	—
Lynn No. 75 Patriot PA506	46	19	200	◒	○	○	◓	◓	○	A,B	a,g	*D*
Archbold 16006	38	21	225	◒	○	○	○	○	○	A,B,D	b,d,g	—
Keller W2-6	27	21	225	◒	◒	○	○	○	○	A,B,D	g	—
Keller W-6	32	18	200	◒	◒	○	○	◓	○	A,B,D	a,d,g	—
Putnam Durable	48	20	200	◒	○	○	○	○	◓	A,D	h	*D*
Archbold 14006	28	19	200	●	○	○	◓	○	○	A,B,D	a,b,g	*F*
Wood, 8-ft.												
Werner W368	78	30	225	◒	○	◓	◉	◒	◒	A,B,D	i	*A*
Keller W2-8	56	30	225	◒	○	○	◓	◒	◒	A,B,D	d,e	—

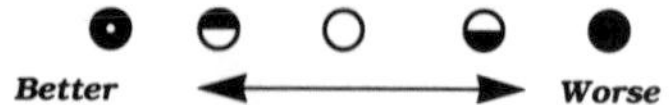

open ladder's front and back legs, the less likely the ladder is to tip.

❼ **Ease of opening and closing.** The panelists opened and closed each ladder several times. Balky hinges, sticky pivots, and such lowered a ladder's score.

❽ **Ease of carrying.** A difference of a pound or two didn't seem to matter to panelists, who carried the ladders closed.

❾ **Ease of moving.** How easily you can pick up an opened ladder and move it a few feet. Light weight, a comfortable handhold, and proper balance were assets panelists looked for.

Specifications and Features

All 6-ft. models: Let you safely stand no more than 3 ft. 7 in. to 3 ft. 10 in. from ground.
All 8-ft. models: Let you safely stand no more than 5 ft. 3 in. to 5 ft. 9 in. from ground.
Except as noted, all models have: Grooves or traction treads on steps to deter slipping.
All wood models have: Steel tie rods under steps for structural integrity.
All aluminum and fiberglass/aluminum models have: Pad at bottom of each leg to protect floors and deter slipping.

Key to Advantages

A— Space between side rails reduces pinching hazard.
B— Spreaders, which hold ladder open, unlikely to pinch fingers
C—Pail shelf has rounded corners. For 6-ft. models, that design judged less hazardous than sharp corners on others; for 8-ft. models, rounded corners matter less, since shelf is $6^1/2$ ft. from floor.
D— Pail shelf folds automatically when ladder closes.
E— Spreaders are protected from damage because they are inside side rails.
F— Has clips to keep folded ladder closed (but clips are easily lost).

Key to Disadvantages

a— Wobbled noticeably without load.
b— Leg bottoms were not horizontal to floor and could damage it.
c— Failed American National Standards Institute test for step-bending.
d— Tested samples had splinters as received.
e— Pail shelf broke when ladder was closing.
f— Pail shelf judged likely to strike you in the face when folding ladder.
g— Pail shelf could strike you in the face when folding ladder, a slight hazard.
h— Spreaders could pinch or squeeze fingers when you're closing the ladder.
i— Truss block, which supports steps, fell out when we tested ladder's ability to withstand severe load.

Key to Comments

A— Top plate or pail shelf accommodates tools.
B— Lacks spreaders; pail shelf keeps ladder open.
C— Has "H"-shaped spreaders with handle; allows ladder to be opened and closed with one hand.
D— Has smooth (not grooved) step surfaces, judged comfortable for standing.
E— Lacks pail shelf.
F— Tie rods under steps judged likely to need tightening more often than on most wood models.
G— Has 5-yr. warranty.
H—Discontinued but may still be available in some Sears retail stores. Replacements as follows: **40116** by **40306**, $20; **42386** by **42176**, $50; **42156** by **42216**, $40; **42388** by **42178**, $80.

Interior Semigloss Paints

Because of its sheen, semigloss paint is a popular choice for woodwork—moldings, baseboards, doors, and windows. And because its shiny surface tends to resist dirt and to endure scrubbing, it's often the best choice for kitchen and bathroom walls, and for working surfaces such as bookshelves and kitchen cabinets.

For the following report, 32 brands of interior semiglosses—21 latex (water-based) and 11 alkyd (oil-based) paints—in white plus five pastel colors, were tested. Paints were taken from the high end of the brand lines, since many low-end paints lack the qualities of hiding power and washability.

The Ratings list the paints in alphabetical order, because no one product is the best choice for every job. However, two paints are check-rated: the alkyd *Pratt & Lambert Cellu-tone* and the latex *Sherwin-Williams Superpaint*, because they performed best over the widest range of colors.

Ratings of Interior Semigloss Paints

Listed by types. Within types, listed alphabetically. Brand-performance judgments apply to all colors within a brand. Dashes indicate that a suitable color wasn't available. Prices are the manufacturer's suggested retail price per gallon, rounded to the nearest dollar.

❶ **Gloss.** Some "semiglosses" were shinier than others. Observed judgments of gloss are divided into three categories. Low (**L**) appeared merely satiny. High (**H**) approached the shininess of a glossy enamel. Medium (**M**) was in between, and is probably the best choice if you're looking for a clear-cut semigloss finish.

❷ **Brushing ease.** Alkyd paints are stickier and thus not as easy to brush on as the latexes.

❸ **Leveling.** A paint that scored well shows a minimum of brush marks when it is dry.

❹ **Sagging.** A judgment of how much a paint may run or "curtain" when applied with a brush.

❺ **Spattering.** Paints that scored well here resisted the tendency to spin paint mist off a roller.

As published in a May 1989 issue of Consumer Reports.

Brand and model	Price	Gloss ❶	Brushing ❷	Leveling ❸	Sagging ❹	Spattering ❺	Resistance to: Scrubbing ❻	Resistance to: Water ❼	Resistance to: Blocking ❽	WHITE: Color name	WHITE: One-coat hiding ❾	WHITE: Two-coat hiding ❾	WHITE: Fading ❿	GOLD: Color name	GOLD: One-coat hiding ❾	GOLD: Two-coat hiding ❾	GOLD: Fading ❿
Alkyd (oil-based)																	
Benjamin Moore Satin Impervo Series 235	$25	L	○	◓	○	◓	◓	◉	◉	White	1	4	○	Golden Glow	3	6	◓
Devoe Velour Series 26XX	27	M	◒	○	○	◓	◉	◉	◉	White	1	4	○	Swirl	5	6	◓
Dutch Boy Dirt Fighter Series 555XX	18	M	○	○	○	◉	◉	◉	◉	Diamond White	2	5	◓	Champagne	3	6	◓
Glidden Spred Lustre Series 4600	27	H	○	○	○	◓	◉	◉	◉	White	1	3	◓	Buttered Rum	2	6	◒
Glidden Spred Ultra Series 4200	30	L	○	◓	○	◓	◉	◉	◉	Bright White	2	5	○	Buttered Rum	2	6	◒
Pittsburgh Wallhide Series 27	26	H	○	◓	○	◉	○	◉	◉	White	1	4	◓	Cactus Flower	2	3	◓
Pratt & Lambert Pro-Hide Plus E3800	21	M	○	◓	○	◓	◉	◉	◉	White	2	5	○	Wind Song	5	6	◓
✓ Pratt & Lambert Cellu-Tone Series C30572	30	L	○	◓	◓	◓	◉	◉	◉	One Coat White	2	6	○	Wind Song	5	6	◓
Sherwin-Williams Classic 99	26	L	○	○	◓	◉	◉	◉	◉	Pure White	2	5	◓	Caramel Corn	3	6	◉
Tru-Test Supreme Satin W-Line	22	L	○	○	◓	○	◉	◉	◉	White	2	5	◒	Sunny Mesa	2	6	○
Valspar Semi-Gloss Enamel Series 614	25	M	○	◒	○	◓	◓	◉	◉	Super White	2	6	◉	Javelin	5	6	◉
Latex (water-based)																	
Benjamin Moore Regal Aquaglo Series 333	23	L	◉	◓	○	◉	◓	○	◉	Non-Yellowing White	2	5	◉	Golden Glow	3	6	○
Devoe Wonder-Tones Interior Series 38XXN	26	H	◉	◒	◓	◓	◉	○	◒	White	2	4	◓	Swirl	2	6	○
Dutch Boy Super Kem-Tone	18	L	◉	○	◓	◉	◓	◒	●	White	1	2	◉	Wheat Grain	4	6	◉
Dutch Boy Dirt Fighter Series 73XX	18	L	◉	◓	◓	◉	◓	◒	●	White	1	2	◉	Champagne	3	6	◉
Dutch Boy (K Mart) Fashion Fresh	14	L	◉	○	◓	○	◓	○	●	White White	1	2	◉	Honeycomb	2	5	◉
Dutch Boy (K Mart) The Fresh Look	18	L	◉	◓	○	①	◉	○	●	White White	1	3	◉	Honeycomb	3	6	◉
Fuller-O'Brien Double AA Series 214XX	21	M	◉	◒	◓	○	◒	◉	◓	White	1	4	◉	Perfect Gold	6	6	◓
Fuller-O'Brien Ful-Flo Series 614XX	25	M	◉	○	○	◓	◉	◉	●	White	2	4	◓	Perfect Gold	2	6	◓
Glidden Spred Enamel Series 3700	21	L	◉	◒	◉	◓	○	○	◉	High Hiding White	1	3	◉	Buttered Rum	2	6	○
Kelly-Moore Acry-Plex Series 1650	24	M	◉	◒	◓	○	◉	◓	◉	White	1	3	◉	Gold	4	6	◉
Lucite Wall & Trim Enamel Series 1699	19	L	◉	◒	◉	◉	◉	○	◉	White	1	3	◉	Natural Beige	2	6	◉
Magicolor Luster Plus Series 4211	18	L	◉	◒	◉	◉	◉	◒	●	Non-Yellowing White	2	4	◉	Spice Beige	5	6	◉
Montgomery Ward Ultra Coat Series 3696②	22	L	◉	○	◉	◒	◉	○	●	White	2	5	◉	Light Coin Gold	2	5	◉
Pittsburgh Satinhide Series 88-00	21	L	◉	○	◓	①	○	○	●	White	1	4	◉	Cactus Flower	1	2	◉
Pratt & Lambert Aqua Satin Series Z32372	26	L	◉	◓	○	◉	◉	○	◉	One Coat White	2	4	◓	Wind Song	3	6	◓
Sears Easy Living Semi-Gloss Series 7100	15	L	◉	◒	◉	◉	◓	○	●	Non-Yellowing White	2	5	◉	Golden Harvest	2	6	◉
Sears Easy Living for a Lifetime Series 7700	20	L	◉	◒	◉	◉	◉	○	●	Pure White	3	6	◉	Golden Harvest	4	6	◉
Sherwin-Williams Classic 99	21	L	◉	◓	○	◉	◓	◓	●	Pure White	1	3	◉	Caramel Corn	2	6	◉
✓ Sherwin-Williams Superpaint	24	L	◉	◓	◓	◒	◉	◉	◉	Pure White	2	6	◉	Caramel Corn	4	6	◉
Tru-Test Supreme E-Z Kare Series EZS	22	L	◉	○	◓	◉	◓	○	◓	White	1	4	◉	Sunny Mesa	2	6	◉
Valspar Acrylic Series 42214	22	L	◉	◒	◓	◉	◉	○	◉	White	2	5	◉	Javelin	3	6	◓

① *Too variable, sample to sample, to spatter.* ② *This brand discontinued in the colors tested.*

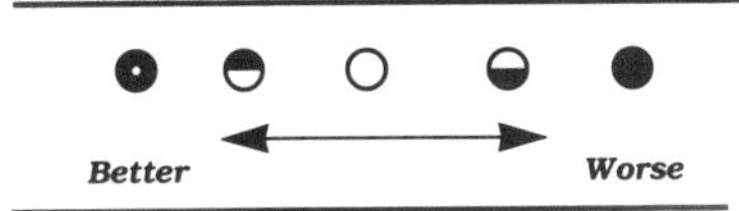

❻ **Scrubbing.** The tougher a paint's dried surface, the more it can resist repeated cleanings.

❼ **Water-resistance.** This measures how impervious to standing water a paint was. Important for surfaces likely to be wetted, such as tabletops, bathroom walls, and plant shelves.

❽ **Blocking.** Blocking is a tendency for paint to stay tacky even after it has dried. More of a problem with latex paints, blocking makes some brands unsuitable for use on working surfaces such as bookshelves and tables.

❾ **Hiding power.** The numbers here correspond to paint concealment (based on a Consumers Union test of rolled-out paints). On a scale of light to dark—or worst to best coverage—1 is light and 6 is dark. The two columns indicate these coverage results after the first and second coats of paint, respectively. Very few paints scored a "6" after only one coat.

❿ **Fading.** How well the individual colors hold up to the bleaching effects of sunlight. The lowest-scoring paints can fade even in indirect sun.

Properties specific to individual colors

PINK				GREEN				BLUE				YELLOW			
Color name	One-coat hiding ❾	Two-coat hiding ❾	Fading ❿	Color name	One-coat hiding ❾	Two-coat hiding ❾	Fading ❿	Color name	One-coat hiding ❾	Two-coat hiding ❾	Fading ❿	Color name	One-coat hiding ❾	Two-coat hiding ❾	Fading ❿
Heathermist	2	6	◓	Green Whisper	2	6	◓	Country Blue	6	6	◓	Chrysanthemum	1	4	◓
Pixie Pink	2	5	◓	Pistachio	2	6	◓	Blue Magic	4	6	◓	Spring Tint	1	3	○
—	—	—	—	Mint Frost	2	6	◓	Crystal Blue	3	6	◓	Sunlight	2	4	◓
Sweet Clover	2	5	◓	Green Ice	2	5	○	Biscayne Blue	3	6	◓	Gin Fizz	1	3	○
Sweet Clover	2	6	○	Green Ice	2	6	◒	Biscayne Blue	5	6	◓	Gin Fizz	2	3	○
Stick Candy	1	5	◉	Frosted Mint	4	6	◉	Danish Blue	3	6	◉	Sugar Cookie	2	4	◓
Rose Mist	2	5	◓	Cool Eve	3	6	◓	Azure Foam	3	6	◓	Celestial Yellow	2	5	◓
Rose Mist	2	5	◓	Cool Eve	4	6	◓	Azure Foam	3	6	◓	Celestial Yellow	2	5	◓
Cotton Candy Pink	2	5	◉	Iceberg Lettuce	3	6	◉	Clearly Blue	4	6	◉	Yellow Primrose	1	2	◓
Orange Blossom	1	3	○	Gossamer Green	2	6	○	Skyline Blue	4	6	○	Lemon Cream	1	2	○
Blush	2	6	◉	Green Haze	4	6	◓	Sky	4	6	◉	Sunshine Yellow	2	4	◉
Heathermist	1	3	◉	Green Whisper	2	6	◉	Country Blue	4	6	◉	Chrysanthemum	2	3	◓
Pixie Pink	2	6	◓	Pistachio	4	6	◓	Blue Magic	5	6	◓	Spring Tint	2	4	○
—	—	—	—	Orient Green	2	5	●	Hazy Blue	3	6	◉	Lemon Yellow	2	5	◓
—	—	—	—	Mint Frost	1	4	●	Crystal Blue	4	6	◉	Sunlight	1	3	○
—	—	—	—	Mint Frost	1	3	◓	Bellflower	2	6	◉	Corn Yellow	1	2	◓
Pink Whisper	2	6	◉	Mimosaceae	1	5	◉	Bellflower	3	6	◉	Yellow Bud	1	3	◉
Pink Ruff	1	2	◉	Marsh	5	6	◉	Heidi	4	6	◉	Marguerite	1	2	◉
Pink Ruff	1	2	◓	Marsh	5	6	◓	Heidi	3	6	◓	Marguerite	1	2	◓
Sweet Clover	1	3	◉	Green Ice	1	3	◉	Biscayne Blue	2	5	◉	Gin Fizz	1	2	◓
Pink	2	6	◉	Green	3	6	◉	Blue	3	6	◉	Yellow	1	3	◓
Rose Pearl	1	3	◉	Spring Green	2	6	◓	Dove Blue	2	6	◉	—	—	—	—
—	—	—	—	Mint Cooler	2	4	◓	Blue Horizon	2	6	◉	Daffodil Yellow	1	4	◓
Pink Cloud	2	6	◉	Light Mint	2	6	◓	Blue Diamond	4	6	◉	Sunflower	1	2	◒
Stick Candy	1	2	◉	Frosted Mint	2	5	◓	Danish Blue	2	6	◉	Sugar Cookie	1	2	◓
Rose Mist	2	5	◓	Cool Eve	3	6	◓	Azure Foam	2	6	◓	Celestial Yellow	2	4	○
Apple Blossom	2	6	◒	Huckleberry Green	4	6	◉	Federal Slate	3	6	◉	Sunflower Yellow	2	4	◓
Apple Blossom	3	6	◒	Huckleberry Green	6	6	◉	Federal Slate	5	6	◉	Sunflower Yellow	2	6	◉
Cotton Candy Pink	1	3	◉	Iceberg Lettuce	2	6	◉	Clearly Blue	3	6	◉	Yellow Primrose	1	3	◓
Cotton Candy Pink	1	3	◉	Iceberg Lettuce	4	6	◉	Clearly Blue	3	6	◉	Yellow Primrose	2	3	◓
Rose Quartz	1	4	◉	Gossamer Green	2	6	◉	Skyline Blue	1	4	◉	Lemon Chiffon	1	2	○
Blush	2	5	◒	Green Haze	2	6	◉	Sky	3	6	◉	Sunshine Yellow	1	4	◓

Finishing Sanders

The tool of choice for giving wood a smooth, satiny surface is a finishing sander, also known as a pad sander. Finishing sanders come in several basic sizes, based on the portion of a standard 9×11-inch sandpaper sheet they hold.

Here's how to use a finishing sander safely and effectively:

- *Use a light touch.* A sander's weight produces enough pressure for the tool to operate properly, so don't apply any pressure yourself. Concentrate on guiding the sander.
- *Keep moving.* Don't keep the tool in one area too long, lest it wear a depression into the surface. Whenever you have to stop sanding, lift the sander from the wood before you turn it off.
- *Sand, don't shape.* If you use a finishing sander to round the corners of a board or to even off a jagged edge, you will most likely punch holes in the sandpaper and eventually damage the padding on the sander's base. Use a wood file or a rasp for that kind of shaping.
- *Use the right sandpaper.* Sandpaper is labeled with a grit number—the lower the number, the coarser the paper. For rough wood stock, start with 40- to 60-grit and use progressively finer grits as the work progresses. Wood you intend to paint can be finished with 150-grit.
- *Clear the air.* Wood dust is not only an annoyance, it has been known to aggravate conditions such as asthma, dermatitis, and allergies. At a minimum, wear a dust mask and vent air away from the work area if you can.

A good sander should let you change sandpaper quickly. It should have some way to deal with dust. And it should be reasonably quiet and easy to control. The 20 sanders in the following Ratings represent the sizes, styles, and brands you'll find at well-stocked hardware stores. Included are low-priced sanders meant for casual use as well as a few more expensive "professional" models.

Ratings of Finishing Sanders

Listed in order of estimated quality. Except where separated by a bold rule, closely ranked models differed little in quality.

❶ **Brand and model.** Moderately priced models for occasional use and more expensive professional models were tested. If you can't find a model, call the company.

❷ **Price.** The manufacturer's suggested retail price. Discounts are common.

❸ **Type.** The **palm** sanders, designed to be guided with one hand, are better suited for experienced users. The **two-handled** models are better for novices because they are less likely to sand depressions into the wood.

❸ **Sheet size.** The part of a standard 9 × 11-inch sheet of sandpaper each sander holds: **quarter-sheet,** about $4^1/_2 \times 5^1/_2$ inches; **one-third-sheet,** about $3^1/_2 \times 9$ inches; **half-sheet,** about $4^1/_2 \times 11$ inches. The **one-sixth-sheet** model takes a sheet about $3^1/_2 \times 4^1/_2$ inches. One-third-sheet models are a good in-between size for all-around work; larger models may not perform well in tight quarters, while the smaller ones have to be moved continuously to sand uniformly.

❺ **Weight.** In ounces, including the cord. Weight only matters when you're working overhead or on a vertical surface; you have to support the sander and hold it against the work.

❻ **Sanding speed.** Shows how rapidly each sander removed wood from pine boards using 100-grit paper. (Sanders that can be switched between orbital and back-and-forth motion were tested in their orbital mode.) The best sander was nearly three times faster than the slowest.

❼ **Clamp quality.** A major point of convenience with any finishing sander. The best clamps open and close easily, have a wide opening, and keep the paper taut and flat against the sander's base.

❽ **Handling.** How easy it was to guide the sander across a board. In tests, some sanders hopped, rotated, or resisted changes in direction.

❾ **Evenness.** It's difficult to sand wood with a wide grain, such as fir. The light parts of the wood are softer than the dark parts and wear away faster. The better models sanded fir plywood without leaving valleys in the softer parts. Sanders with lower scores left noticeable valleys.

❿ **Noise.** The better the score, the quieter the sander. The loudest exceeded 90 decibels, a level that Consumers Union testers believe requires hearing protection.

⓫ **Vibration.** The assessment of each sander's ability to minimize the vibration you'll feel when you use the tool. The worst will leave your hands tingling.

⓬ **Pad contact.** How evenly each sander's pad contacted the surface being sanded. A low score means that a large part of the pad did not touch the surface, increasing the possibility of sanding unevenly. In actual practice, if the sandpaper is tight and the sander kept in constant motion, pad contact won't matter much.

⓭ **Cord length.** The longer the power cord the better, provided the cord isn't so stiff it impedes your ability to move the sander across the wood. Models with particularly good or bad cords are noted in the Advantages and Disadvantages.

As published in a September 1990 issue of Consumer Reports.

❶ Brand and model	Price ❷	Type ❸	Sheet size ❹	Weight ❺	Sanding speed ❻	Clamp quality ❼	Handling ❽	Evenness ❾	Noise ❿	Vibration ⓫	Pad contact ⓬	Cord length ⓭	Advantages	Disadvantages	Comments
Black & Decker 4011	$ 79	Palm	1/4	47 oz.	◓	◉	◓	◒	○	◉	◓	96 in.	A,B,D,G,I,J,K	—	A,D
Black & Decker 7458	122	2-handled	1/2	64	◓	◉	○	◒	○	○	●	72	A,D,E,F,K	c,q,t,v	B,F
Hitachi SV12SA	80	Palm	1/4	47	◒	◉	○	○	○	◉	◒	100	F,J	—	A
Makita B04550	86	Palm	1/4	37	◒	◒	◉	○	○	◒	◓	74	A,B,D,F,J	—	B,H
Sears Craftsman 11602	33	Palm	1/4	40	◓	◓	○	○	◒	○	●	96	F,H	i	A,B
Skil 7582	121	2-handled	1/3	71	◉	○	◓	◒	◓	◒	◓	96	J	a,g,j,v	B,C
Black & Decker 7448	47	2-handled	1/3	37	◓	◓	◓	◒	◒	○	◓	72	I	a,v,w	B,F
Ryobi S500A	79	Palm	1/6	42	◒	◓	◒	◒	◓	◓	○	79	F,J	a,n	—
Makita 9035	112	2-handled	1/3	56	◒	◉	◒	○	◓	◒	◓	82	I,J	a,m,v,w	B,H
Skil 7382	69	2-handled	1/3	55	◓	◒	○	○	○	◒	◒	60	C,D	a,l,m,r,s,t,w	B
Milwaukee 6016	84	Palm	1/4	46	○	◓	○	●	◒	○	●	105	F,H	o,t,w	B,E
Skil 7575	70	Palm	1/4	43	◒	◒	○	◒	○	◓	◉	96	F,I,J	d,v	B
Skil 7576	78	Palm	1/4	43	◒	◒	○	◒	○	◒	◓	96	A,B,D,I,J	b,d,v	B
Ryobi S600	90	Palm	1/4	46	●	○	◉	●	◓	○	◉	80	J	k,v	G
Sears Craftsman 11611	23	2-handled	1/3	50	○	●	○	○	◒	○	●	72	F,H	a,e,n,s	B,I
Ryobi LS35	98	2-handled	1/3	54	◒	◒	○	○	◓	◓	●	80	J	a,g,m,p,w	—
Sears Craftsman 11616	67	2-handled	1/2	83	○	●	◒	◉	●	●	○	122	C,D,H,L	e,i,k,l,n,s,t,u	B,D
Porter-Cable 330	97	Palm	1/4	61	●	◒	◓	◒	◓	◉	◉	82	I,J	d,f,i,k,v	B
Sears Craftsman 11613	55	2-handled	1/3	67	◒	●	◒	◓	●	●	●	72	C,D,F,H,L	a,e,i,l,n,p,s,t,u	B,D
Wen 300	50	2-handled	1/3	54	◒	●	◒	◒	○	◒	◒	71	J,L	a,d,h,i,j,k,v,x	B,I

Specifications and Features

All: Run on 120 volts and are double-insulated. *Except as noted, all:* • Use only orbital motion. • Lack provision for dust collection. • Can sand to within 1/8-in. of perpendicular edge on at least one side. • Have rocker or toggle On/Off switch that's easy to operate but poorly marked. • Have easily used finger-operated clamps to hold paper; clamps tend to pull paper taut as they close. • Come with good instruction manual. • Have reasonably limp power cord, which doesn't interfere with work. • Judged suitable for use with self-adhesive sandpaper. • Can be used on wood, metal, and plastics, or to remove paint. • Have one-yr. warranty against defects in noncommercial use.

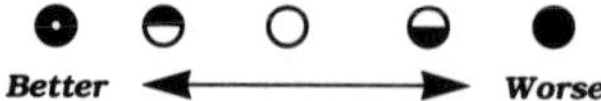

Key to Advantages

A— Has through-the-paper dust collection; requires punching holes in paper with tool provided.
B— Paper punch cuts all holes at once, with paper on sander.
C— Has dust-collecting skirt around base.
D— Has dust-collecting bag.
E— Variable speed.
F— Sands to within less than 1/8-in. of perpendicular edge on front and sides.
G— User can replace motor brushes without disassembling sander.
H— On/Off switch has better markings than most.
I— Power cord limper than most; less likely to interfere with sander's motion across work.
J— Judged more suitable than most for repairs by user.
K— Instructions better than most.
L— Has switch to convert sander from orbital to straight-line motion.

Key to Disadvantages

a— Uses 1/3 or 1/6 of standard sandpaper sheet; often requires measuring to cut sheet to proper size.
b— Punch for dust-collecting system doesn't perforate paper cleanly.
c— Punch cuts only one hole at a time in sandpaper.
d— Harder to load paper than most.
e— Clamps do not tend to tighten paper.
f— Clamps require tool to operate easily.
g— Clamps require strong fingers to operate.
h— Sandpaper must be folded to fit into clamps.
i— Clamps protrude from base far enough to scratch adjacent vertical edge of work.
j— Instructions worse than most.
k— Sanded no closer than 1/8 to 3/8-in. from adjacent perpendicular edge.
l— Dust-collecting skirt must be removed to get sander close to adjacent perpendicular edge.
m—On/Off trigger switch requires two operations to lock sander on. Judged hard for left-handed persons to use.
n— On/Off switch harder to operate than most.
o— On/Off switch more likely than most to be operated by accident.
p— Front handle judged too small for people with large hands to control easily.
q— Front handle judged too large for people with small hands to control easily.
r— Front handle judged too low for good control when using sander at arm's length.
s— Main handle judged too low for good control when using sander at arm's length.
t— Power cord stiffer than most; could interfere with sander's motion.
u— Dust-collecting bag not securely fastened to sander.
v— Judged unsuitable for use with self-adhesive paper.
w— Instructions judged only fair.
x— Levers to switch from orbital to straight-line sanding confusingly marked.

Key to Comments

A— Round base available as option (not tested).
B— Instructions don't recommend users replace motor brushes.
C— Instructions cover more than one sander.
D— Optional dust-collecting system allows sander to be connected to vacuum cleaner; can be useful for people sensitive to wood dust, but may make sander awkward to use.
E— Has unlimited warranty against defects in non-commercial use.
F— Has two-yr. warranty against defects.
G— Instructions say to use sander on wood only.
H—According to instructions, motor brushes are self-limiting; when brushes wear out, the motor won't run, preventing major damage to motor.
I— Discontinued. (**Wen 300** may still be available in some stores.)

Exterior Trim Paints

Although many homeowners prefer neutral and pastel colors for their houses, they often prefer vivid colors for their doors, windows, shutters, and the like. This report on trim paints concentrates on vibrant and deep shades: blazing reds, deep blues, glowing yellows, rich greens, chocolate browns, glistening blacks, and the whitest of the whites. Paints tested range in luster from flat to high gloss, with a few steps in between; prices vary from $10 to $30 a gallon.

In all, some 38 brands were tested: 26 latex (water-based) and 12 alkyd (oil-based) paints. Do-it-yourselfers favor latex because it's easy to work with, dries fast, and cleans up with soap and water. Alkyd paints can't be applied to a damp surface; they can take several days to dry hard; and you have to use mineral spirits for cleanup or to thin the paint. But latex paints are inferior to alkyds for smoothness, toughness, adhesion, and other key properties.

No paint is perfect. You won't find any one type or brand that excels in every respect and in every color. Invariably, you have to accept some tradeoffs.

Ratings of Exterior Trim Paints

Listed by types; within types, listed alphabetically. Brand-related properties apply to all colors tested for a brand. Color-related properties apply to a color. Dashes mean a suitable color wasn't available.

❶ **Brand and model.** If you can't find one of these paints, call the company.

❷ **Price.** In most cases, the manufacturer's approximate retail price per gallon. A * indicates the price paid.

As published in a September 1990 issue of Consumer Reports.

❸ **Gloss.** The descriptions here are based on Consumers Union measurements. Flat (**F**) is the dullest, followed by eggshell (**EG**), satin (**S**), semi-gloss (**SG**), gloss (**G**), and high gloss (**HG**).

❹ **Brushing ease.** Alkyd formulations have improved over the years, but they're still harder to apply than latex paints.

❺ **Leveling.** If you want a smooth finish, look to the alkyds.

❻ **Sagging.** How well a paint resisted the tendency to run, drip, or sag like a curtain.

❼ **Adhesion.** Each paint was applied to weathered panels that had been coated with a paint formulated to "chalk." When the panels had dried thoroughly, Consumers Union testers scratched them and pressed tape over the scratch to see how much paint would pull away. But any of these paints should

❶ Brand and model	❷ Price	❸ Gloss	❹ Brushing ease	❺ Leveling	❻ Sagging	❼ Adhesion	❽ Blocking	White ❾ Hiding	White ❿ Color change	White ⓫ Chalking	White ⓬ Mildew	White ⓭ Dirt	Black ❾ Hiding	Black ❿ Color change	Black ⓬ Mildew	Black ⓭ Dirt	Brown ❾ Hiding	Brown ❿ Color change	Brown ⓬ Mildew	Brown ⓭ Dirt
	Brand-related properties																			
Alkyd (oil-based)																				
Devoe All-Weather Gloss (Series 1XX)	$32	SG	◒	◓	●	◉	◉	◓	◉	◓	○	○	◉	◒	◓	◉	◉	●	◓	◉
Devoe Velour Semi-Gloss (Series 29XX)	34	SG	○	◓	●	◉	◉	—	—	—	—	—	—	—	—	—	—	—	—	—
Dutch Boy Dirt Fighter Gloss (Series 1XX-2XX)	25	G	○	○	○	◉	◉	○	◉	◓	○	○	◉	◒	◓	◓	◉	●	◉	◉
Fuller O'Brien Weather King (Series 660-XX)	28	G	○	○	○	◉	◉	◓	◓	◉	◒	◒	◉	◒	◓	◉	◉	●	◓	◉
Glidden Spred House Dura-Gloss (Series 19XX)	27*	G	○	○	○	◉	◉	○	◓	◓	◒	○	◉	◒	◉	○	◉	●	◓	◓
Moore's High Gloss (130)	26	SG	◓	◓	◒	◉	◉	◉	◓	○	◉	◉	—	—	—	—	—	—	—	—
Moore's High Gloss Enamelized (Series 110)	24	③	◓	○	○	◉	◉	○	◓	○	◓	◉	◉	○	◓	◉	◉	●	◓	◓
Pittsburgh Sun-Proof Gloss (1 line)	31	G	○	○	○	◉	◉	◒	○	◉	○	○	—	—	—	—	◉	●	○	◓
Pratt & Lambert Effecto High Gloss (E31172)⑤	36	HG	○	◓	●	◉	◉	◒	◉	◉	●	◒	◉	◓	◉	◉	◉	●	◓	◉
Pratt & Lambert Permalize Gloss (C34972)⑤	31	G	○	◓	◒	◉	◉	◒	◓	◓	◒	○	◉	◓	◉	◉	◉	●	○	◓
Sears Best Weatherbeater Gloss (Series 4800)	23	SG	○	◓	○	◉	◉	◓	◓	◓	○	◒	—	—	—	—	◉	●	○	◓
Valspar Gloss (Series 2XX)	27	HG	○	○	◒	◉	◉	○	◓	◉	●	◒	◉	◒	◓	◓	◉	●	◓	◓
Latex (water-based)																				
Ameritone Enamelized (W2500)	25	SG	◉	●	◉	●	●	◓	◉	◉	◉	●	◉	◓	◉	◉	◉	◓	◉	◉
Benjamin Moore Moorgard (Series 103)	20	EG	◉	●	◉	◉	◉	◉	◉	◉	◉	◒	◉	◉	◉	◉	◉	◓	◓	◉
Benjamin Moore Moorglo (Series 096)	22	S	◉	●	◓	◉	◉	◓	◉	◉	◉	◒	◉	○	◓	○	◉	○	◉	○
Devoe Wonder Shield (Series 18XX)	28	SG	◉	◒	◓	●	●	○	◉	◉	◉	●	◉	◓	◉	◉	◉	○	◓	◓
Devoe Regency Satin (Series 19XX)	28	F	◉	◒	◓	●	○	—	—	—	—	—	—	—	—	—	—	—	—	—
Dutch Boy Dirt Fighter Gloss (Series 19XX)	21	SG	◉	●	◉	●	◓	○	◉	◉	◉	●	—	—	—	—	◉	○	◉	◓
Dutch Boy Super Gloss (Series 74XX)	23	SG	◉	●	◉	●	●	◒	◉	◉	◉	●	◉	◓	◉	◓	◉	◓	◉	◓
Dutch Boy Super Satin (Series 77XX)	22	EG	◉	●	◓	●	●	○	◉	◉	◉	◒	◉	◉	◉	◓	◉	◉	◉	◓
Fuller O'Brien Versaflex Gloss (Series 615-XX)	30	G	◉	●	◉	●	●	—	—	—	—	—	—	—	—	—	—	—	—	—
Fuller O'Brien Weather King (Series 664-XX)	27	SG	◉	◒	◉	●	◒	◉	◉	◉	◉	●	◉	◉	◉	◓	◉	◓	◉	◓
Glidden Spred House Dura-Gloss (Series 39XX)	21*	SG	◉	◒	◓	●	●	◉	◉	◉	◉	◒	◉	◉	◉	◓	◉	◉	◉	◉
Glidden Spred House Dura-Satin (Series 29XX)	21*	EG	◉	◒	◓	●	●	◉	◉	◉	◉	◒	—	—	—	—	◉	◉	◉	◉
Lucite Enamel Gloss (Series 18XX)	18*	SG	◉	●	◓	●	◒	◒	◉	◉	◉	●	◉	◓	◉	◓	◉	◓	◉	◉
Lucite Satin (Series 22XX)	17*	S	◉	●	◉	◒	●	○	◉	◉	◉	●	—	—	—	—	—	—	—	—
Pittsburgh Manor Hall Eggshell (79 Line)	30	F	◉	◒	◉	◒	●	○	◉	◉	◉	◒	◉	◓	◉	◉	◉	◓	◉	◓
Pittsburgh Sun-Proof Semi-Gloss (78 Line)	26	SG	◉	●	◉	●	◒	◉	◉	◉	◉	◒	◉	◉	◉	◉	◉	◓	◉	◓
Pratt & Lambert Aqua Royal Satin (Z3002)⑤	29	SG	◉	●	◉	●	◒	◉	◉	◉	◉	◒	◉	◓	◉	◓	◉	◓	◉	◓
Sears Best Weatherbeater Satin (Series 5100)	20	EG	◉	○	○	●	●	◉	◉	◉	◉	◒	◉	◓	◉	◉	◉	○	◉	◓
Sears House Shield (Series 2800)	10	F	◉	○	○	●	◉	○	◉	○	◉	○	◉	◒	◉	◓	◉	◒	◉	◉
Sears Weatherbeater Premium Satin (Series 4700)	16	EG	◉	●	◉	●	◓	◓	◉	◉	◉	○	◉	◓	◉	◓	◉	○	◉	◓
Sears Weatherbeater Premium Semi-Gloss (Series 5000)	17	SG	◉	●	◓	●	◓	◉	◉	◉	◉	●	◉	◉	◉	◓	◉	◉	◉	◓
Sherwin-Williams A-100 Satin (A82 Series)	21	EG	◉	●	◉	●	◒	◓	◉	◉	◓	◒	◉	◓	◉	◉	◉	◓	◉	◉
Sherwin-Williams Superpaint Gloss (A84 Series)	25	SG	◉	●	◉	●	●	◉	◉	◉	◉	●	—	—	—	—	◉	◓	◉	◓
Tru-Test Supreme Accent Color Semi-Gloss (AG Line)	24	SG	◉	●	◉	●	●	—	—	—	—	—	—	—	—	—	◉	◓	◉	◉
Tru-Test Supreme Weatherall Gloss (GHP Line)	24	SG	◉	◒	◓	●	●	◓	◉	◉	◉	●	◉	◒	◉	◉	—	—	—	—
Valspar Semi-Gloss (Series 43XX)	24	S	◉	●	◓	◓	●	◓	◉	◉	◉	◒	◉	○	◉	◓	◉	◓	◉	◓

① *Tends to erode rapidly when exposed to the weather.* ② *Brighter than most yellows.* ③ *Gloss too variable to rate.* ④ *Grayer than most blues.*

◉ ◓ ○ ◒ ●

Better ←——→ *Worse*

adhere well to new surfaces or to properly prepared old paint.

❽ **Blocking.** Paint, especially latex paint, can remain tacky long after it dries. The lower the score here, the more likely the paint will stick to things that touch it.

❾ **Hiding.** A ◉ means the paint should cover almost any previous color in one coat. ◓ means the paint should cover in one coat if the old color doesn't contrast sharply with the new. Paints judged ○ should cover a similar color in one coat, a darker color in two. Paints judged ◒ or ● will require at least two coats to cover a similar color.

❿ **Color change.** How individual colors stand up to the elements. The scores take into account fading, yellowing (for whites), and loss of gloss.

⓫ **Chalking.** White paints with the lower scores chalked the most. They might be preferable in cities or suburbs, where dirt and pollution can quickly soil white paint.

⓬ **Mildew.** How well a paint resists the buildup of mildew. No paint will eliminate existing mildew; that requires washing.

⓭ **Dirt.** The faster a paint dries, and the smoother and more tack-free its surface, the less dirt it will attract.

Color-related properties

Red				Green				Blue				Yellow			
Hiding ❾	Color Change ❿	Mildew ⓬	Dirt ⓭	Hiding ❾	Color Change ❿	Mildew ⓬	Dirt ⓭	Hiding ❾	Color Change ❿	Mildew ⓬	Dirt ⓭	Hiding ❾	Color Change ❿	Mildew ⓬	Dirt ⓭
—	—	—	—	◉	●	◓	◉	—	—	—	—	—	—	—	—
●①	●	◒	◓	—	—	—	—	◉	●	◓	◓	●②	●	●	◒
—	—	—	—	—	—	—	—	◉	●	○	◓	—	—	—	—
—	—	—	—	◉	●	◓	◉					○	●	○	◒
—	—	—	—	◉	●	◓	◓	—	—	—	—	—	—	—	—
—	—	—	—	—	—	—	—	—	—	—	—	—	—	—	—
—	—	—	—	◉	◒	◓	◓	—	—	—	—	—	—	—	—
○①	◉	◒	◓	◉	●	○	◓	◉④	●	◒	◓	●	●	◒	○
●①	○	●	◓	◉	●	◓	◉	◉	●	◓	◉	●②	●	●	◒
—	—	—	—	◉	○	◓	◓	—	—	—	—	—	—	—	—
—	—	—	—	—	—	—	—	—	—	—	—	—	—	—	—
●①	○	●	○	◉	●	○	◉	◉	●	●	◓	●②	●	●	◒
—	—	—	—	—	—	—	—	—	—	—	—	●②	◒	◉	●
—	—	—	—	—	—	—	—	◉	◉	◉	○	●②	◓	◓	◒
○①	●	◓	◒	◓	◉	◓	○	◓	◓	◉	○	●②	◓	◓	◒
—	—	—	—	◉	◓	◓	○	—	—	—	—	—	—	—	—
●①	◓	◉	◓	—	—	—	—	●①	◉	◉	◓	●②	◉	◉	○
—	—	—	—	—	—	—	—	◉	◓	◉	◒	○	◓	◉	●
—	—	—	—	—	—	—	—	◉	◓	◉	○	—	—	—	—
—	—	—	—	—	—	—	—	◉	◓	◉	◓	◒	◉	◉	◒
●①	◉	◉	○	—	—	—	—	◉	◉	◉	◓	◒②	●	◉	●
—	—	—	—	◉	◓	◉	◓	—	—	—	—	◒	◒	◉	●
—	—	—	—	◉	◉	◉	◓	—	—	—	—	◉	◒	◉	◒
—	—	—	—	◉	◉	◉	◓	—	—	—	—	◉	○	◉	○
—	—	—	—	—	—	—	—	—	—	—	—	—	—	—	—
—	—	—	—	—	—	—	—	—	—	—	—	—	—	—	—
—	—	—	—	●	○	◉	◓	◉④	◓	◉	●	◒	○	◉	○
—	—	—	—	○	◓	◉	◓	◉④	◉	◉	◒	●	◓	◉	●
—	—	—	—	◉	◓	◉	○	—	—	—	—	—	—	—	—
—	—	—	—	◉	◓	◉	◓	◉	○	◉	◓	—	—	—	—
—	—	—	—	◓①	○	◉	◓	◉①④	●	◉	◓	—	—	—	—
—	—	—	—	◓	◓	◉	◓	◉④	◓	◉	◓	—	—	—	—
—	—	—	—	◓	◓	◉	◓	◉④	◓	◉	○	—	—	—	—
—	—	—	—	◉	◓	◉	◉	—	—	—	—	●	◓	◓	○
—	—	—	—	◉	◉	◉	○	—	—	—	—	◒	◓	◉	●
●①	◉	◉	◓	◉	○	◉	○	◓	○	◉	◒	◒②	◒	◉	●
—	—	—	—	—	—	—	—	—	—	—	—	—	—	—	—
●①	◒	◉	○	◉	◓	◉	◓	◉	◓	◉	◓	◒②	◒	◉	◒

⑤ *Product number of white only.*

Names of colors tested

Alkyd paints

Devoe All-Weather Gloss: White, Black, Dark Brown, Forest Green. **Devoe Velour Semi-Gloss:** Hot Tango 2VR2A (red), Blue Saga 1BL11A, Dynamo 1BY26A (yellow). **Dutch Boy Dirt Fighter Gloss:** Gloss White, Black, Cocoa Brown, Triple Blue. **Fuller O'Brien Weather King:** White, Black, Sealskin (brown), Meadow Green, Sunray (yellow). **Glidden Spred House Dura-Gloss:** White, Black, Stratford Brown, Crylight Green. **Moore's High Gloss:** Brilliant White. **Moore's High Gloss Enamelized:** Outside White, Black, Tudor Brown, Chrome Green. **Pittsburgh Sun-Proof Gloss:** White, Bahama Brown, Colonial Red, Kentucky Green, Blue Mood, French Lacquer (yellow). **Pratt & Lambert Effecto:** High Hiding White, Black-Gloss, Leather Brown, Grenadier Red, Dublin Green, Postal Blue, Canary Yellow. **Pratt & Lambert Permalize:** High Hiding White, Black, London Brown, Glen Green. **Sears Best Weatherbeater:** White, Barcelona Brown. **Valspar:** Non-Chalking White, Black, Chocolate Brown, Cranberry (red), Forest Green, Blue (custom-mixed), Yellow (custom-mixed).

Latex paints

Ameritone: White, Black, Spanish Brown, Lustre Glow 1D39C (yellow). **Benjamin Moore Moorgard:** Brilliant White, Black, Tudor Brown, Blue 791, Yellow 321. **Benjamin Moore Moorglo:** White, Black, Tudor Brown, Tartan Red, Chrome Green, Blue 791, Yellow 321. **Devoe Wonder Shield:** White, Black, Dark Brown, Forest Green. **Devoe Regency Satin:** Hot Tango 2VR2A (red), Blue Saga 1BL11A, Dynamo 1BY26A (yellow). **Dutch Boy Dirt Fighter:** White, Cocoa Brown, Triple Blue, Pawnee (yellow). **Dutch Boy Super Gloss:** White, Gloss Black, Cocoa Brown, Triple Blue. **Dutch Boy Super Satin:** White, Black, Cocoa Brown, Triple Blue, Pawnee (yellow). **Fuller O'Brien Versaflex Gloss:** Bright Red, National Blue, Sunshine (yellow). **Fuller O'Brien Weather King:** White, Black, Seal Skin (Brown), Meadow Green, Sunray (yellow). **Glidden Spred House Dura-Gloss:** White, Black, Stratford Brown, Crylight Green, Victorian Yellow. **Glidden Spred House Dura-Satin:** White, Stratford Brown, Crylight Green, Victorian Yellow. **Lucite Enamel Gloss:** White, Black, Bark Brown. **Lucite Satin:** White. **Pittsburgh Manor Hall:** Super White, Ebony Black, Bahama Brown, Kentucky Green, Blue Mood, French Lacquer (yellow). **Pittsburgh Sun-Proof:** White, Black, Bahama Brown, Kentucky Green, Blue Mood, French Lacquer (yellow). **Pratt & Lambert:** White, Black, London Brown, Glen Green. **Sears Best Weatherbeater:** White, Molten Black, Barcelona Brown, Mowbray Hunt Green, Tiber River Blue. **Sears House Shield:** White, Molten Black, Barcelona Brown, Desert Palm (green), Daring Indigo (blue). **Sears Weatherbeater Premium Satin:** White, Molten Black, Barcelona Brown, Azalea Leaf (green), Daring Indigo (blue). **Sears Weatherbeater Premium Semi-Gloss:** White, Molten Black, Barcelona Brown, Azalea Leaf (green), Daring Indigo (blue). **Sherwin-Williams A-100:** White, Tricorn Black, Chateau Brown, Mown Grass (green), Yellow Corn. **Sherwin-Williams Superpaint:** Super White, Chateau Brown, Mown Grass (green), Yellow Corn. **Tru-Test Supreme:** Tru-Brown, Tru-Red, Tru-Green, Tru-Blue, Tru-Yellow. **Tru-Test Supreme Weatherall:** White, Black. **Valspar:** White, Black, Chocolate Brown, Cranberry (red), Forest Green, Dominion Blue, Oleo Yellow.

Waterproofing Paints

The surest but most expensive cures for a wet basement involve excavation to direct the water away from the house. You don't always have to resort to such drastic measures, though. If the basement walls in your house are merely damp, a couple of coats of waterproofing paint may be the most sensible cure. The water will still be outside, pressing to get in, but the paint can hold it at bay.

Painting concrete walls is not as easy or as cheap as painting the living room, nor are the results as predictable. Waterproofing basement walls entails lots of tedious, messy work. And because a gallon of waterproofing paint covers a much smaller area than a gallon of ordinary wall paint, the cost of materials is high. Finally, the choice of paint is crucial to success. A few of the 16 paints tested allowed very little water to leak through, but several others did poorly.

Don't expect these paints to be the ultimate cure for a wet basement. The paints can alleviate dampness or mild seepage, not outright leakage. You may well want the advice of a house inspector or a contractor before you buy some.

Ratings of Waterproofing Paints

⊙ ◓ ○ ◒ ●

Better ◄——► *Worse*

Listed in order of estimated quality, based on water resistance.

❶ **Brand and model.** Most are available only in white; footnotes list the exceptions. If more than one color was available, both white and beige were tested.

❷ **Type.** The oil-based epoxy liquids **(OEL)** have to be mixed with the catalyst provided and applied within 30 minutes or they become too thick to use. The oil-based liquids **(OL)** come ready to use but should only be applied to dry walls because oil does not adhere to water. Cementlike powders **(P)** have to be mixed with water; if you mix more than you can apply in about 4 hours, the paint hardens in the pail. The powders are best applied to a wet wall. Water-based liquids **(WL)** are the easiest to use; they are ready-mixed and can be brushed onto damp or dry walls. Water-based epoxy **(WEL)**, like the other epoxies, must be mixed with a catalyst.

❸ **Price.** The manufacturer's suggested retail price, rounded to the nearest dollar. These paints are rarely on sale. + means shipping is extra.

❹ **Size.** Only the weight of the powders is listed. It's hard to say how many gallons of paint they can make because the amount of water to be added varies with each brand.

❺ **Cost for sample basement.** An estimate, rounded to the nearest $25, of what it costs to apply two coats to 1120 square feet of concrete wall. These paints are generally comparable in price to interior wall paint, but a gallon doesn't go as far since it has to cover a rough, pitted surface.

❻ **Water resistance.** The bars in the graph show how waterproof these paints were. To measure water resistance, testers at Consumers Union put two coats of paint on concrete blocks, sealed the openings in each block, then suspended a water tank 8 feet overhead; tubing from the tank let water flow into the cavities, to simulate the water pressure exerted at the bottom of a typical basement wall. The condition of the blocks was checked periodically, and the water tank was weighed to find out how much water was seeping through the paint. Statisticians analyzed the leakage-rate data to produce the index of water resistance shown here.

❼ **Ease of application.** How easy it was to apply each paint, using a short, stiff-bristled brush. Waterproofing paints are much harder to work with than wall paints because you must apply them with a stabbing or scrubbing motion to seal all the pin-sized holes in concrete blocks.

❽ **Stain removal.** How easily a grease stain could be removed from a painted block, using a soft brush and an all-purpose household cleaner.

❾ **Surface smoothness.** The smoothest felt like standard wall paint; the roughest, like a concrete driveway. Rough walls may not matter if you use your basement for storage only, but you may want a nicer finish if the basement serves as a living space.

As published in a February 1990 issue of Consumer Reports.

❶ Brand and model	❷ Type	❸ Price	❹ Size	❺ Cost of sample basement	❻ Water resistance (0 20 40 60 80 100)	❼ Ease of application	❽ Stain removal	❾ Surface smoothness
✓ **Barrier System Cat. No. 502 Epoxy Resin**①②	OEL	$41+	5 qt.③	$500		○	⊙	⊙
✓ **Atlas Epoxybond Epoxy Waterproof Sealant**①	OEL	54	3 qt.③	825		◒	⊙	⊙
Glidden Spred Waterproof Basement Paint④	OL	15	1 gal.	350		○	●	○
Bondex Waterproof Cement Paint④	OL	21	1 gal.	475		◓	◒	◒
Tru-Test Supreme Tru-Seal Waterproofing Masonry Paint④	OL	18	1 gal.	400		◓	◒	⊙
UGL Drylok Masonry Waterproofer	OL	18	1 gal.	400		◓	◒	◒
Moore's Waterproofing Masonry Paint⑤	OL	18	1 gal.	400		◓	◒	⊙
Thoro Super Thoroseal Redi-Mix Liquid④	OL	57	2 gal.	625		◓	◒	●
Thoro Super Thoroseal④	P	29	20 lb.	675		◓	●	●
Quikrete Heavy Duty Masonry Coating	P	12	40 lb.	150		●	●	●
Bondex Waterproof Cement Paint	P	19	25 lb.	100		◒	●	○
UGL Drylok Double Duty Sealer④	P	26	35 lb.	350		◓	●	●
Quikrete Waterproofing Masonry Coating	P	10	20 lb.	225		◓	●	●
Muralo Tite Vinyl Latex Waterproofing Paint	WL	15	1 gal.	350		⊙	⊙	●
Sears Basement Waterproofing Latex Wall Paint (Series 5640)	WL	11+	1 gal.	250		⊙	⊙	●
Not Acceptable								
■ *The following product was judged Not Acceptable because of extremely poor water resistance.*								
Sears Dry Living Aqua Poxy (Series 5616)	WEL	27+	1 gal.⑥	550		⊙	○	⊙

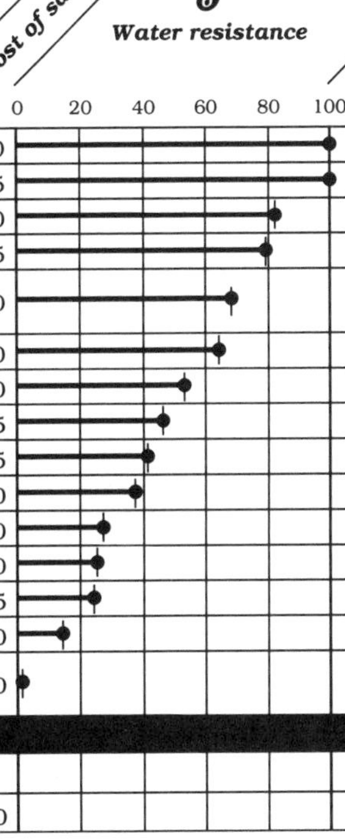

① *Available only as clear sealer. Manufacturer of* ***Atlas*** *says product can be tinted slightly.*
② *Available from Defender Indo, P.O. Box 820, New Rochelle, N.Y. 10801-0820.*
③ *Includes catalyst.*
④ *Available in white only.*
⑤ *Available in white only. Manufacturer says product can be tinted.*
⑥ *Includes catalyst and filler.*

Cordless Screwdrivers

Driving screws for an hour or so with a standard screwdriver can be torture, even for the most adept do-it-yourselfer. A power tool—a cordless screwdriver, to be precise—does the work faster and easier.

Introduced only a couple of years ago, the cordless screwdriver is now the best-selling battery-powered tool. It appeals not only to professionals who must drive lots of screws every day, but also to ordinary homeowners who want a tool that will save some elbow grease. The cordless screwdriver is a not-too-distant relative of the cordless drill, a more versatile but more expensive tool. Some do-it-yourselfers can get by with one or the other, others use both.

"Professional" or "contractor" screwdrivers, which sell for $100 and up, have the feel of a precision tool. They're typically light in weight to minimize fatigue. They often have two worthwhile features. One is an adjustable clutch, which stops the bit from turning once the screw is driven far enough and so provides precise control. The other is a removable battery pack. If you buy a second pack, you can keep one pack on charge while working with the other.

Lower-priced screwdrivers, marketed to homeowners and hobbyists, are meant for light-duty, off-and-on jobs around the house. They usually aren't as solidly constructed as the typical professional model, even though they may have more power. If a hobbyist screwdriver has an adjustable clutch (few do), it may not be as sturdy as the one on a pro model. Typically, the cheaper screwdrivers come with a charging stand instead of a removable battery pack; they often can be left in the stand and so stay fully charged between uses. But when the batteries run down, you have to wait several hours for them to recharge. The worst homeowner models, priced at $20 to $50, are often skimpily constructed—you might think some were toys.

The 18 cordless screwdrivers tested include both professional and hobbyist models.

Ratings of Cordless Screwdrivers

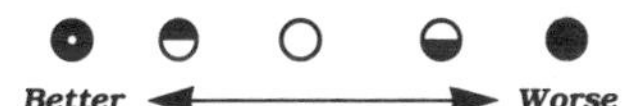

Listed in order of estimated quality. Except where separated by bold rules, differences between closely ranked models were slight. "Professional" models are footnoted.

❶ **Price.** Manufacturer's suggested retail price, rounded to the nearest dollar.

❷ **Shape.** Pistol-shaped models **(Ps)** resemble an electric drill. Pencil-shaped models **(Pn)** look like a fat version of an ordinary screwdriver. Convertible models **(C)** have a movable handle that lets them take either pencil or pistol shape.

❸ **Weight.** To the nearest ¼ pound, not including battery charger.

❹ **Bit sizes.** The manufacturer's designation (or an estimate by Consumers Union noted with *, when no bit size was given) for the bits supplied. Each Phillips bit should fit either a small (number 1) or a medium (number 2) slot. Each slotted bit matches a screw of a particular diameter—a number 8 bit fits a number 8 screw, for example—or at least it's supposed to. Replacement bits are widely available.

❺ **Torque.** Using a precise electric brake called a dynamometer, testers at Consumers Union measured the maximum twisting motion (torque) each screwdriver could exert before stalling. The dynamometer automatically increased the load on a screwdriver at a controlled rate until stalling occurred. Then the load was reduced at the same rate and the procedure was repeated to see if the tool performed consistently. This test also gave an indication of how much power the batteries could deliver on a full charge. Screwdrivers judged 0 or better should have enough power for general work.

❻ **Sustained power.** Each tool was operated continuously to learn how long it could deliver 1C inch-pounds of torque. The *Skil Twist 2105* couldn't deliver that much torque; it was tested at 5 inch-pounds.

❼ **Handling.** A composite judgment that includes handle comfort, trigger position and response, and the presence or absence of a clutch. (A clutch stops the bit but allows the motor to keep running once the screw is driven all the way. Models with no clutch can drive a screw too far.)

❽ **Bit quality.** Generally mediocre. Consumers Union downgraded models supplied with bits that weren't properly finished, shaped, or sized.

❾ **Charging time.** How many hours each unit needs in order to take on a full charge.

As published in an August 1989 issue of Consumer Reports.

Brand and model	*Price* ❶	*Shape* ❷	*Weight, lb.* ❸	❹ *Bit sizes* *Phillips*	*Slotted*	*Torque* ❺	*Sustained power* ❻	*Handling* ❼	*Bit quality* ❽	❾ *Charging time, hr.*	*Advantages*	*Disadvantages*	*Comments*
Skil 2305	$44	Ps	1½	2*	8*	⊙	⊙	⊙	○	3	B,H,I,J	f	*B*
Black & Decker 9025	64	Ps	1½	1*,2*	6*,8*	⊙	◓	◓	◓	16	B	c	*A*
Black & Decker 9034	30	Pn	1	2	8–10	◓	○	◓	◓	12	B,D,H	—	*A,G*
Wen 226	25	Ps	1¼	2,3	8,10	◓	○	○	◓	3	B,I	a,d,e,h	—
Milwaukee 6539-1①	108	C	1	1*,2*	7*	○	●	⊙	◓	1	A,C,D,E,J	c	*D*
AEG EZ502①	108	C	1	1*,2*	7*	○	●	⊙	◓	1	A,B,C,D,E,J	c	*D*
Skil Super Twist 2210	42	Pn	1	2*	8*	◓	◒	◓	◒	3	B,D,G,I	d	*A*
Stanley 75-050	50	Ps	1¾	2	8	◓	◓	◒	◒	3,12	B,C,D,F,G	a,h	*D*
Makita 6720DW①	72	Pn	¾	2	6*	◒	●	◓	⊙	3	—	f	*B*
Ryobi BD-10R①	82	Pn	¾	1*	8*	◓	◒	◓	●	3	A,G,J	e,h	*B*
Black & Decker 9018	35	Pn	1	2	8–10	◒	●	◓	○	12	B,H	g	*A*
Skil Twist 2105	29	Pn	¾	2*	7*	●	●	○	◓	5	B,H	d,g,h,k	*A*
Sears Craftsman 11120	22	Ps	1	1,2	5,7	◒	●	◒	○	3	D,H,I	b,h,i	*A,F,H*
Sears Craftsman 11123	20	Pn	1	1,2	5,7	◒	●	◒	◓	3	D,H,I	b,d	*A,E,H*
Houseworks MES-133C	18	Ps	¾	2*	8*	◒	●	●	◓	12	D	a,f,h,i,j	*B*
Not Acceptable													
■ *The following models were judged Not Acceptable because they broke when tested as a manual screwdriver and could no longer be used.*													
Sears Craftsman 11124	36	Ps	1¼	1,2	5,7	⊙	○	◒	○	3	A,D,G,I	j	*A,F,H*
Lady's Mate 803-W-1	49	C	¾	1*,2*	5*,6*	◒	●	○	⊙	12	A,D,J	j	*A,C*
Alltrade 794-S-1	49	C	1	1,2	6,8	●	●	○	○	12	A,C,J	f,j	*B*

① *"Professional" model.*

Key to Advantages

A—Has adjustable clutch.
B—Can be left on continuous charge.
C—Removable battery pack.
D—Has charge-indicator lamp.
E—Has full-charge indicator.
F—Has dual-speed charging.
G—Bits can be stored on screwdriver.
H—Has manual collet lock to prevent shaft from turning.
I—Trigger response judged better than most.
J—Trigger lock judged better than most.

Key to Disadvantages

a— Lacks collect lock.
b— Collet lock does not prevent shaft from turning.
c— Trigger response judged worse than most.
d— Lacks safety lock-out for trigger.
e— Screwdriver repeatedly fell out of wall-mounted charger stand.
f— No storage provision for bits.
g— Balance judged worse than most.
h— Handle design judged worse than most.
i— Trigger location judged worse than most.
j— Bit fell out of collet when screwdriver was pointed bit-down **(Sears Craftsman 11124)** or when screwdriver was inverted and shaken **(Houseworks, Lady's Mate, Alltrade)**.
k—Would not sustain 10 inch-pounds of torque.

Key to Comments

A— Charging stand can be wall-mounted.
B— Has no charging stand.
C— Model tested is pink; **804-W-1** is blue.
D— Transformer at charging stand.
E— Output shaft of driver is offset from centerline of screwdriver.
F— Has wrist strap.
G— Discontinued; no longer available. According to manufacturer, model will be replaced by one with more power and other features.
H— Manufacturer provides no information on whether unit can be left on continuous charge.

Index